THE
POLITICAL
ECONOMY OF
CORRUPTION
IN CHINA

Studies on Contemporary China

Studies on Contemporary China

THE POLITICAL ECONOMY OF CORRUPTION IN CHINA

JULIA KWONG

An East Gate Book

M.E. Sharpe
Armonk, New York
London, England

An East Gate Book

Copyright © 1997 by M.E. Sharpe, Inc.

Library of Congress Cataloging-in-Publication Data

Kwong, Julia.
The political economy of corruption in China / Julia Kwong.
    p.   cm.
"An East Gate book."
Includes bibliographical references.
ISBN 0-7656-0086-2 (cloth : alk. paper).—ISBN 0-7656-0087-0 (pbk : alk. paper)
1. Political corruption—China.   2. China—Politics and government—1949—
I. Title.
JQ1509.5.C6K96   1997
320.951—dc21
97-13320
CIP

Printed in the United States of America

The paper used in this publication meets the minimum requirements of the
American National Standard for Information Sciences—
Permanence of Paper for Printed Library Materials,
ANSI Z 39.48-1984.

BM (c)   10   9   8   7   6   5   4   3   2   1
BM (p)   10   9   8   7   6   5   4   3   2   1

Contents

Preface

There were numerous reports in the Chinese and foreign press on the abuse of power by state officials at every level in the late seventies and eighties, but I had never experienced it personally on my many visits to China until 1989. On this trip, a Chinese friend who worked at a university secured me accommodation in a metropolitan center by giving the hotel manager a box of imported chocolate. On the same trip, I was offered the opportunity to make some money by buying a television set and other electrical appliances from the Friendship Store, a prerogative accorded to foreign visitors at the time; my contact would supply the buyers, and I would make about 300 yuan on each piece. During a discussion of collaborative research, an academic colleague suggested that his wife visit North America as one of the conditions.

These acts may not be clearcut manifestations of corruption but they are certainly inappropriate from a Western point of view. Such improprieties from fellow academics whom I had held in high regard over the years shocked me. True, they were looking after my interests and the means used were not necessarily illegal, but their actions were disturbing especially given the puritanical standards once held in Communist China, where cadres were criticized for eating a few peanuts owned by the state and were expected to sacrifice everything for the collective. If these academics, traditionally regarded as icons and custodians of morality in Chinese society, would so openly make such offers to make money and personal gains, I realized that perhaps corruption had become widespread and a regular part of Chinese life.

While this study on corruption stemmed from my personal encounters in the late eighties, my interest extends beyond understanding its proliferation in that particular period. Scholars, such as Jean Oi and Connie Squires Meaney, have examined corruption in rural and urban settings, and Alan P.L. Liu has analyzed reports in the *Renmin Ribao* to understand the different forms of corruption in the eighties. More recently, Ting Gong studied corruption as the outcome of changes in the government's developmental policies. My approach is historical; it is only through a diachronic approach that one can obtain a clear understanding of corruption in contemporary China. I traced the evolution of corruption from 1949, when the Communist Party took power, to 1989, when it became so widespread as to elicit popular protest culminating in the June 4 Tian'anmen Incident. I examined how the close symbiotic relationship between politics and economics bore its imprint on corruption.

In the seventies, when China first opened its doors to outsiders, visitors found a safe society where the owners of items left behind were traced and the articles returned. Even political refugees from China agreed with this description of an honest society. Those old enough to appreciate the events of the fifties were euphoric at the memory of the days when government officials were honest and committed. These accounts stood in stark contrast to the experiences of many recent visitors. Some were robbed or had their pockets picked; others paid state officials fees illegitimately imposed. The questions are: Are the descriptions of these earlier periods accurate? If they are, what contributed to honest governance in the earlier period? How was the situation undermined? What prompted the changes in the eighties?

Visitors in China have witnessed an overall increase in crimes, but I shall only focus on the growth of corruption. Corruption is breaking the rules of a society, and yet we often impose the rules of one society to evaluate another. Social scientists condemn the extent to which officials in developing countries breach Western standards of permissible social exchanges, and regard Third World societies as corrupt. Likewise, I was upset with my Chinese friends who probably saw nothing wrong in giving gifts and getting favors.

The norms governing the limitations of acceptable behavior in Western and Third World societies are dissimilar. These contextual differences have to be taken into account in any study of corruption. Furthermore, China is not only a Third World country but has been for a long time a strictly socialist one. The highly valued principle of private ownership in Western societies is condemned and this form of ownership largely legislated out of existence in socialist countries. Consequently, to define corruption in the Western tradition as the privatization of public property is inappropriate. It cannot capture the mutated forms of corruption when public goods are not pocketed but only put to personal use. A customized version that takes into account the local context and at the same time is compatible with the essence of the generally accepted social science definitions of corruption is needed here.

In chapter 1, I grappled with the meaning of corruption. Since this study focused on state employees and since the ruling group in any society legitimizes social conduct and sets the limits on proscribed behavior, I examined the legal and administrative pronouncements that represented the dominant views of Chinese society on the matter. The legal code outlined narrow and behaviorally identifiable criteria of corruption to guide the behavior of the general public, whereas the rules of conduct provided by the Chinese government as the largest if not the sole employer specified expectations for almost all of the country's working adults. I explored the meanings of corruption at these two levels and the changes in interpretations over time. From a plethora of nuances and meanings of corruption, I developed a simple generic definition: Corruption is breaking legal and organizational rules to use public goods or the power vested in one's public office for private ends. In short, it is the exchange of power for personal benefits.

Chapter 2 provided a useful background for readers not familiar with Chinese social development and delineated the backdrop necessary to understanding corruption in that country. The forty years between 1949 and 1989 coincided with the transition from socialism to the introduction of limited forms of market economy. These changes were incremental, but for the purpose of my analysis I used the death of Mao Zedong in 1976 to divide these years into two broad periods and highlighted features of the political economy out of the welter of details in the social milieu, the premise being that the larger political economy impinged on the work organization to influence the behavior of the administrative staff in the state bureaucracy.

Chapters 3 and 4 examined the different dimensions of corruption—the incidence, the monetary value, the kinds of goods exchanged, the strategies used, and individual and organizational corruption. Official announcements and statistics provided only limited information. Consequently, I culled reports in the two national newspapers, the *Renmin Ribao* and the *Guangming Ribao,* and a local one, the *Sichuan Ribao,* for the period between 1949 and 1989 to obtain a more elaborate picture. These data were further supplemented by materials released by the Chinese government in the late eighties and early nineties, publications in Hong Kong and Taiwan, and from interviews with Chinese immigrants in North America and members of the Hong Kong business community trading with China. A clear picture of the development of corruption during these forty years gradually emerged by piecing together information from these eclectic sources.

Chapter 3 took a synchronic approach and examined how the socialist features of Chinese society shaped corruption in the economic sector. It identified three basic characteristics of communist governments and showed how the domination of the Communist Party, the lack of private ownership, and the absence of free markets produced popular forms of gray corruption, such as administrators' breaking organizational rules to benefit the work unit or enjoying state property on the job. Chapter 4 took a diachronic approach looking at the changes in corruption over time. Although the incidence of corruption, the monetary values involved, and the proportion of individual corruption increased over the years, there was no dramatic change in the kinds of goods traded. However, fraud, speculation, and other means one generally associated with illicit strategies used in the market economy became more common.

The pre-1976 Chinese society characterized by a low level of production, a high concentration of power at the top, and a weak formal criminal justice system had a lower incidence of corruption than the post-1976 society, with higher production, better standards of living, greater local authority, and a more institutionalized criminal justice system. The trend observed here challenges the popular wisdom that attributes corruption to the lack of resources, a high concentration of power, and the absence of a strong criminal justice system. Thus, I sought an explanation to these changes in the shifting political economy of the society.

Chapter 5 pulled together the different observations to provide a theoretical understanding of corruption in socialist China. The answer offered is not dissimilar to John Hagan's power control theory, which attributed crimes to the differential power relations in the economic structure. Corruption is committed by those in power. While Hagan focussed on the managers' power location in the organization, I ventured beyond its boundary to seek an explanation in the structure of the political economy. Administrators are always given more power than their subordinates. Vesting power in administrators is unavoidable in the functioning of any bureaucracy but this power can also be used as capital to exchange for goods and opportunities for their personal benefits. The propensity for this to happen rests not just on the conditions within the organizations, but changes in the political economy which structure the opportunities and constraints within the organizations. I used the transition from socialism to market socialism in China between 1949 and 1989 to illustrate how these structural changes shaped the authority and prerogative of state officials in the workplace and how the concomitant cultural changes shaped the ambience within the organizations. The specific congeries of these different forces within and outside the work organizations provide different opportunities and constraints, as well as moral restraints and incentives, for corruption, which in turn explains the evolution of and differences in corruption between the classical socialist and the market socialist period in China.

Acknowledgments

I would like to express my gratitude to all the individuals who helped me in the preparation of this book. They are too numerous to mention here, and some who shared information with me, no doubt, prefer to remain anonymous. Russell Smandych, Maria Los, and Elizabeth Comack introduced me to the criminology literature. Ko Kwai Fun helped me in collecting the data. Lawrence Douglas, Rick Linden, and Nicholas Tavuchis read chapters of the earlier drafts and gave me helpful comments. Shirley Quinn translated my Chinese-English into English.

The Social Sciences and Humanities Research Council of Canada generously funded this project. The Fairbank Center of East Asian Studies of Harvard University, the Universities Services Center of the Chinese University of Hong Kong, and the James Dickinson Library of the University of Nevada, Las Vegas, provided me access to their research facilities. The University of Manitoba, my home institution, facilitated the preparation of this manuscript in more ways than one.

Finally, my greatest debt is to Victor who has always supported in every way all my academic endeavors.

Measurement Equivalents

1 hectare = 2.471 acre
1 jin/catty = 1 1/8 pound
1 mu = 0.165 acre
1 yuan = about U.S.$ 0.30 to 0.50

THE
POLITICAL
ECONOMY OF
CORRUPTION
IN CHINA

1

The Meanings of Corruption

The popular Chinese word for corruption is *tanwu;* the two characters literally mean greed and dirt, which conjure up the image of depravity. The Chinese abhorrence for corruption is even more evident when this term is used in conjunction with *fuhua* or *fubai* to describe a corrupt individual, government, or society. *Fuhua* literally means rotten and decomposed, and *fubai,* rot and nonperformance. The government language is more sober and sanitized than these colorful everyday communications, but the official position on corruption is unequivocal. *Yichuan mou shi,* meaning using one's power or authority for private ends, and *jia gong ji si,* meaning to use public resources to manufacture private ones, provide behavioral definitions, but these terms too imply selfishness. Even in its more euphemistic official parlance, corruption is still *bu zheng zhi feng,* meaning wrong or devious ways.

The Chinese society, like other societies, condemns corruption. Despite the general condemnation of such behavior, however, the specific actions that constitute corruption in each society are not necessarily the same. There might be universal categories of "right" and "wrong," but the specifics of these cultural categories are shaped by the unique confluence of the peculiarities of the political, economic, and social milieu of each society. Corruption is after all a transgression of norms, and societal norms vary so that what is acceptable in one society may not be tolerated in another.

Generally, socialist values are more rigid and puritanical than capitalist ones. Corruption, as implied in the earlier official definitions of *yichuan mou shi* or *jia gong ji si* is premised on the dichotomy between the public and the private. Authority and resources are vested in one's public position; using them for personal ends is wrong. In a socialist society where private property is eliminated or severely curtailed, the public realm is much broader than in a capitalist society. It is, therefore, easy for an individual to transgress socialist rules and infringe on public interests. Furthermore, many socialist systems have emerged from the need of developing societies to control scarce resources and hasten economic development. In their zeal to direct these resources toward national goals, they vigilantly guard them from falling into private hands. For example, trade and commerce are legitimate private engagements in a capitalist society, but under socialism these activities are state prerogatives. Deriving personal profit from trade is considered wrong. In the importance given to the collective interest, even those enjoying the fruits of their own labor can be denounced as bourgeois—witness the prosecution of merchants, especially wealthy ones, and the confiscation of their properties in the early years of Chinese Communist rule.

Moreover, China still retains some vestiges of tradition found in Third World countries, where the boundaries between public and private realms are blurred. In the past, a country, a province, or a district may have been considered the personal property of an individual or family. In these personalized politics, the prerogatives of the ruler over the ruled were much broader than in modern societies, with their institutionalized checks and balances in governance. One of these Chinese traditions is *nuo yong,* the right of local officials to use public funds under their trust for personal purposes as long as they eventually return the money. In China's feudal past, local officials did not receive guaranteed subventions from the emperor. Their living allowances and government operating budgets came from local collections, and the officials had great discretion in the disposition of these sums.[1] Communist officials continued to enjoy this convenience even though they received salaries and the practical reasons for *nuo yong* had disappeared. Between 1949 and 1979, officials could *nuo yong* public funds with relative impunity. But by 1985 the conditions became more restrictive and the "loan" period was limited to six months; those not returning the money could receive a maximum of seven years imprisonment. In 1988, state employees could borrow public funds for three months and those not repaying within this time would receive penalties similar to those for *tanwu* or embezzlement in the legal context.

Just as societies may have different standards of behavior, so may their guidelines for appropriate practices change over time.[2] The clash of values between generations lends testimony to these subtle changes in the standards of behavior. In the developing countries, the globalization of world economies, with countries drawn more tightly than ever before in their trade relations and cultural interchanges, has produced values and norms that come to resemble more closely those of the industrialized world. The fall of the Eastern European Communist governments in the eighties and the subsequent introduction of market economies there have further accelerated the process of homogenization between socialist and capitalist countries. The Chinese Communist government has maintained its power, but it too has incorporated the market in its central plan. So although the country retains many of its traditions, its cultural and economic systems look more like those of the West today than they did a decade ago. Such changes cannot but modify the values and norms of that society and the meaning it attaches to corruption.

All these point to the uniqueness of corruption in different social and temporal contexts. China, as a socialist and developing country with four thousand years of tradition, has developed its own constantly evolving set of criteria to evaluate corruption. *Nuo yong* is only one of a large number of official prerogatives but it suffices to show the diverse normative standards that can be used. Chinese officials control a wide array of power and resources that can be abused and subject to ingenious forms of misappropriation. The propriety of each action is open to different judgments that can change over time.

Legal and Organizational Codes of Conduct

To understand what corruption means in the Chinese context during the period 1949–1989, one has to examine Chinese legal and organizational rules. These rules govern access to, and the use of, state roles, resources, and power. They offer more precise and stable guidelines of behavior than subjective formulations and judgments of private individuals.[3]

The legal code in any country is a form of social control to safeguard the interests of the dominant group. It is drafted by the ruling group and embodies its ideology, but laws also reflect the prevalent culture. The values of a society are not homogeneous; not all the members share the same values. But laws are meant to be kept. No government can exercise political authority when its legislation is widely opposed and systematically ignored without raising questions on its effectiveness and ability to rule. As a consequence, the legal codes on corruption are carefully crafted documents embodying not only the official ideology but also accepted social attitudes.

Laws proscribe actions that may undermine government authority and legitimize punishments meted out to those who have challenged its power. The death penalty imposed for treason most dramatically demonstrates the legal mandate for eliminating potential threats. Although not as lethal to national security, corruption and widespread malfeasance weaken government legitimacy and effectiveness. Consequently, government must anticipate the different forms of corruption, outlaw such behavior, and attach penalties to transgressions.

The Chinese government, as custodian of a developing country, has an additional reason to punish corruption. In 1949, China was emerging from years of foreign aggression and civil war. The country was devastated and poor, with a per capita annual income that even by 1989 never surpassed 1,178 yuan (about U.S.$500).[4] Officials who made wrong decisions in the deployment of resources, let alone those who used state assets for their own enjoyment, were seen as depriving the nation of valuable inputs for development. This line of thinking has prompted the government sometimes to inveigh against waste, corruption, and bureaucratic behavior that disregarded local needs and conditions in the same directive.[5]

When the Chinese Communist leaders came to power in 1949,

they rejected the Qing and Goumindang legal systems as feudalistic and bourgeois, and entrusted justice personnel to draft a new legal code that would better reflect their political philosophy. In 1952, the government promulgated the Statute of Penalties for Corruption (*tanwu*) which together with the Statute on Counterrevolutionary Crimes remained the only two public legal documents on criminal justice for more than two decades. During the rectification campaign in the wake of the Hundred Flowers Movement, when academics and intellectuals voiced their dissatisfaction with the government, the authors of legal reform were criticized for bourgeois leanings and insubordination to party leadership. In 1957, after twenty-two revisions their draft document was shelved and the ministry of justice dissolved.[6]

It was not until 1979 that a more comprehensive criminal code was promulgated. Crimes were divided into eight categories: (1) counterrevolutionary activities, (2) public security, (3) socialist economic order, (4) personal and democratic rights, (5) property, (6) social order, (7) marriage and family, and (8) dereliction of duties. Supplementary regulations, such as Several Answers to the Application of Law Relating to Economic Crimes (1985) and Supplementary Regulations Relating to Corruption (*tanwu*) and Bribery (1988) were introduced in the eighties. But the 1979 code has remained the basic document on criminal justice in China.

When laws are written in broad and general language to anticipate every eventuality and bind the behavior of the whole population, administrative codes of conduct are necessary to provide details about the proscribed conduct of narrower groups such as the state employees. The administrative codes referred to here are not the 1989 administrative laws/code (*xingzheng fa*) that legitimize appeals or provide public recourse to challenge unreasonable government decisions. They are the behavioral guidelines for members of state organizations and describe situations specific to these units. The specifics in these documents add texture to an otherwise formalistic interpretation of corruption provided by the law. Moreover, the legal code provides only an inventory of proscribed behavior and prescribed punishments to warn would-be perpetrators and to guide the prosecution of transgressors. In contrast, the organizational codes are proactive, serving not only to warn members but also to describe expected behavior, giving details of desirable characteristics. These expectations for the ideal incumbent serve a useful foil to examine their opposite—corruption in the organization.

Unlike the West with its public and private formal organizations, all formal organizations in China are public, subject to government regulation and supervision. Even so-called "nongovernment" or grass-roots organizations are closely tied to the state. The State Council oversees all government departments, and its behavioral guidelines have to be adhered to by all state employees. On October 23, 1957, it announced the Regulations on Reward and Punishment of State Administrative Personnel.[7] Just as in the legal field, there was an almost thirty-year hiatus before another set of regulations was disseminated in 1982. On September 13, 1988, the State Council promulgated the Provisional Regulations on the Penalties for Corruption and Bribery of State Administrative Personnel.[8]

Below the State Council, each state department has its own set of regulations. With the institutionalization of law and order in the late seventies and eighties, government units became more diligent in developing and revising their own rules to meet the needs of the changing work environment. Not all of these documents are accessible to public scrutiny, but those that are available provide further interesting details as to what constitutes corruption.

In China, not all state employees are Communist Party members. Nevertheless, the Communist Party plays such an important role in state governance that its role cannot be ignored. It provides directions to state policies, supervises state operations, and, more often than not, intervenes directly in everyday matters. The Chinese Communist Party constitution governs the conduct of its members, who are found in all levels of every state department. The constitution, promulgated for the first time in 1957, was revised in 1969, 1973, 1980, 1982, and 1987, but the expectations for party members remained relatively consistent.[9] The Party's code of conduct complements and reinforces the administrative ones, but it imposes higher standards of moral behavior that go beyond abstaining from corruption. Party members are expected to be righteous, abstemious, altruistic, and self-sacrificing. They are to exhibit exemplary behavior at all times. On February 29, 1980, the party published *Guidelines for the Political Life of the Party*. This code coming so closely after the promulgation of the 1979 criminal code, no doubt was meant to reinforce the legal message and reflect the close cooperation between the Party and other state organs.

Agents of Corruption

The 1952 statute on *tanwu* dealt with "employees of state departments, schools or other subordinate departments" who indulged in corruption. The subjects of *tanwu,* according to article 155 of the 1979 criminal code, were state employees who took property under their trust. According to both documents, only state employees including those working in schools were prosecuted for *tanwu* in China. This might suggest that those likely to be charged for this crime would be far fewer in China than in the West, where anyone holding public office can be held liable. This might be the case in 1952, but by the mid-fifties China was a socialist country with an intrusive government that managed almost every aspect of an individual's life. Aside from maintaining law and order, collecting taxes, and providing social services, the government was also involved in producing and distributing goods for society. Except for the peasants working on the land, almost every salaried working Chinese adult is a state employee.

When the nationalization of industry and the collectivization of agriculture were completed in 1958, the number of state employees soared from sixteen million, or 64 percent of the nonagricultural workers in 1952, to fifty-two million, or 98 percent of the nonagricultural working adults.[10] Article 83 of the 1979 criminal code specified that state personnel were all those working in "state organs, enterprises, and institutions, and other personnel engaged in public service. . . ."[11] Thus, government, business,

service, and social service sectors were all included. Private ownership was introduced in the eighties, but joint ventures and private
enterprises employed less than 0.001 percent of the labor force in
1989.[12] The fact that workers in both the civil service and much of
the economic sector were all state employees makes the Western
distinction between political and economic corruption irrelevant.[13]

The economic sector, however, can be differentiated according to
the diverse forms of public ownership in this socialist country.
Some work in state enterprises, and others in collectives. State enterprises are owned by all members of society, and their workers
are considered state employees; the collectives belong only to the
members of the collective unit, and those working in these units are
not considered state workers.[14] This distinction also applies to peasants farming the collective land, who have never been considered
state workers; only those employed at the commune level receiving
state salaries are state workers. The July 8, 1985, document, Several
Answers to the Application of Laws Relating to Economic Crimes*
acknowledged this class of civil servants working for the collective
units who were "entrusted with responsibilities by the peoples' organizations."[15] The following analysis will not make the distinction
between administrators working for state or collective organizations, because while the state employees may have more security,
administrators in the collective organizations, especially the rural
cadres, have comparable if not more power.[16]

A new category of state personnel was added in the eighties.
With the devolution of fiscal and economic responsibilities, some
production units no longer received guaranteed income from the
state but had to live with the consequences of profit or loss. Sometimes the running of these factories or companies were contracted
out to individuals. The 1988 Supplementary Regulations Relating to
Corruption (*tanwu*) and Bribery covered these "other personnel who
control or administer public property." They did not own factories
or businesses, which remained state or collective properties, but

---

*In socialist countries, economic crimes generally refer to all activities incon-
sistent with the ideologically sanctioned mode of economic organization.

they were more like contractors; like state employees, they could be prosecuted for corruption.[17]

The 1952 statute on corruption and the 1979 criminal code were binding on employees working at all levels of state governance (including those in the economic sector), and the rules of the Communist Party governed the conduct of all its members. However, the state bureaucracy had separate rules for incumbents in different positions. For instance, the March 8, 1952, Decisions on the Handling of Corruption, Wastage, and Bureaucratism, the October 23, 1957, Regulations on Reward and Punishment of State Administrative Personnel, the 1982 State Council Work Regulations, and the September 13, 1988, Provisional Regulations on the Penalties for Corruption and Bribery of State Administrative Personnel were aimed at the administrative staff. And some organizations have their own rules for their personnel as well.

In the West, administrators generally enjoy high status, and the term *ganbu,* or cadres, used for administrators in Chinese everyday language also carries the connotation of power and status. But in the Chinese civil service, twenty-six of the thirty grades fall into the administrative rank; only the last four are of the service/worker rank.[18] The 1982 legal supplement, Decision to Severely Punish Criminals Seriously Undermining the Economy, gave the clearest demarcation of this broad meaning of administrative staff by specifying that these state regulations governed the behavior of administrative and not service/production personnel. Since the administrative personnel, or *xingzheng renyuan,* defined as such covers such a broad category of workers, they do not enjoy the same prestige or influence as those in the West— they are located at all levels of government and in all branches of the state, and are not necessarily highly positioned. Furthermore, personnel within this rank may not be "doing administration" as we understand it in the West, but may be involved in technical work such as engineering, sales, accounting, or simply clerical work. Only the *lingdao ganbu* (leading cadres) or *xingzheng ganbu* (administrative cadres) enjoy prestige and power, *yiban ganbu* (ordinary cadres) do not have such privileges. Still, the repeated laws and regulations against corruption aimed specifically at administrators suggest that this category has more state resources under its jurisdiction And among this broad category of administrators, the administrative personnel have greater power than the technical ones.[19] and are more likely to be guilty of corruption. Therefore this group is the focus of my attention.

Essence of Corruption

The April 21, 1952, Statute of Penalties for Corruption (*tanwu*) provided an exhaustive list of corrupt behavior—"the seizure (*qintun*), theft (*daoqie*), fraud (*pianqu*), or appropriation (*taoqu*) of state property, using extortion (*qiangsuo*) to obtain another's property, accepting bribes (*shouhui lu*), and any other activities that use one's position to benefit oneself (*jiagong ji si*)." Western legal scholars would find this statute, based on a moral interdiction against encroaching on state and other people's private property, crude. But the final catchall phrase, *jiagong ji si,* defines the concept clearly enough. Under this statute, officials who have crossed the boundaries separating the public from the private are guilty of corruption —an offense against property. They used the advantages derived from their public positions to benefit themselves by taking over public or private property and making it their own.

Tanwu has a much narrower meaning in the 1979 legal documents than in the 1952 statute. One can appreciate this semantic change by placing it against the backdrop of Chinese legal reforms. By 1979, the 1952 generic definition of *tanwu* was no longer adequate from a legal standpoint. The term had to be refined to adapt to a criminal justice system increasingly patterned on that of the West, which demands concrete guidelines, tangible proof, and clear evidence in conviction. With this metamorphosis in the criminal justice system, corruption meant only embezzlement from the state. *Tanwu* in article 155 of the 1979 criminal code came under the section on property crime, which referred to state employees stealing public property (not private property) under their trust. It read: "State personnel who take advantage of their office to engage in *tanwu* involving articles of public property are to be sentenced to not more than five years of fixed term imprisonment or criminal detention."[20] The 1988 Supplementary Regulations Relating to Corruption (*tanwu*) and Bribery made the distinction between encroaching on public property and encroaching on private property more explicit. The first referred to state employees' appropriating public property and the second to their extorting property from private sources.

Other crimes of corruption listed in the 1952 statute were found elsewhere in the 1979 legal code. Seizure of property, theft, extortion, and fraud were cited in articles 150 to 153. This is because the 1979 code was aimed at a wider clientele; these crimes against property could be committed even by persons not holding public office. Bribery and confiscation of private property were treated as dereliction of duty under article 185.

Despite this evolution in the usage of *tanwu* in legal documents, and regardless of whether or not one adopts the broader 1952 or the narrower 1979 interpretation, the essence of what constitutes corruption remains the same. Corruption in China is the use of the power or resources endowed by one's official position to benefit oneself, and is consistent with the widely accepted Western definition of corruption as the violation of formal rules by members of an organization to benefit themselves.[21] This definition of corruption is premised on the dichotomy between public and private. In modern societies, the two arenas are distinct. Anyone transferring his/her private property to the public is considered altruistic, but anyone moving public property into one's private realm is considered wrong. China too is a modern bureaucratic state. There is a clear separation between what is public and what is private. Power and privileges supposedly come from holding official positions and not from one's ancestry or particularistic ties. The prerogatives vested in the incumbents of public positions are guided and circumscribed by formal rules. Public property should remain in the public realm. Neither should a public official use his/her position to take over another's private possessions. When state personnel break these rules and use their position to benefit themselves, transferring public or private property for their personal benefits, they are guilty of corruption.

Forms of Corruption Identified in the Legal Codes

Given the different moral standards, values, and economic organization of the capitalist and the socialist systems, the actions that are proscribed and the forms corruption takes in the two systems are not identical. In China, there are as many forms of corruption as there are rules forbidding such actions. I shall examine here only the examples cited as corruption in the central government legal documents. These are seizure (*qintun*), theft (*daoqie*), fraud (*pianqu*), misappropriation (*taoqu*), extortion (*suohui*), bribery (*shouhui*), embezzlement (*tanwu*), smuggling (*zousi*), and speculation (*touji daoba*).

I have shown earlier how "appropriation" is a close but not satisfactory translation of *nuo yong*. The same caution should be applied to the translations used here. While the Chinese meanings are similar to their English translations, they also have their unique connotations. Because simply superimposing our Western understanding can distort their meaning, I shall examine each term in the Chinese context, except for *nuo yong* and embezzlement, which were discussed in an earlier section.

Qintun is the seizing of other people's property. According to the 1979 criminal code, it can be committed by individuals in either their private or public capacities. As in the rest of the proscribed acts to be discussed, however, I am referring specifically to those acts committed by state employees. *Qintun* occurs most often when one person or party is more powerful than another, and the former imposes its will on the weaker. It is common in developing countries where the rule of law is weak. Throughout Chinese history, local officials held inordinate power, and corrupt ones took what they wanted from the powerless populace. Victims were too afraid to resist, but when they did, the officials resorted to force—*qintun* accompanied by physical violence became *daoqie* (robbery/ larceny).

Pianqu, or *zhapian* (fraud), is the intentional perversion of truth for the purpose of inducing another to part with his/her personal belongings. *Taoqu,* a term that appeared in the 1952 statute, has a similar meaning, but it is no longer popular. Chinese officials had great powers and would simply demand what they wanted from their subordinates or charges who were ignorant of their rights, but these same officials would have to file misleading or false reports misrepresenting themselves or their organizational achievements to obtain materials or recompense they were not entitled to from their superiors.

Shouhui (bribery) is receiving anything of value in the discharge of one's duties beyond what is stipulated in the official guidelines. *Shouhui* is when state employees accept but do not actively solicit such payments; *suohui* (extortion) is when they actively demand these illicit rewards by threatening to or actually do withhold services or materials to which their clients are entitled, if their requests are not granted. Like *qintun, suohui* or extortion occurs less frequently in the urban areas, than in the rural areas where the influence of the central government is weak, the powers of the local officials is strong, and state employees are often the sole dispenser of goods or services.

Touji daoba (speculation) is buying and selling goods in ways that produce unreasonable profits. What constitutes reasonable profit is subject to debate and fluctuates over time; for a long time, the Chinese government definition of speculation certainly did not coincide with that in the West. It is difficult to identify the acceptable rate of such returns in China, but perhaps the 5 percent interest paid to owners of confiscated property in the early fifties provide some indication of the official perception at that time. Soon after, the Communist government outlawed private trade, branding anyone engaged in such activities guilty of speculation. Distrust in commerce has its roots in tradition as well as in communist ideology. Traditional Chinese culture placed a high status on farming; merchants were the lowest rung of the occupational scale after scholars, farmers, and workers. Furthermore, Marxism has always placed a premium on production rather than on the circulation of goods.[22] Before 1976, the Chinese Communists regarded trade as the hallmark of capitalism; however, their attitude changed in the open economic climate of the late seventies. Trading outside state jurisdiction was no longer considered speculation. Profit making was not only tolerated but even encouraged. Nonetheless, those who made profits through simply trading goods without adding value to them by processing could still expose themselves to accusations of price gouging.

Smugglers (*zousi fan*) in the West generally are those who move contraband or goods across national borders without paying the required duties.[23] Again, the Chinese definition of smuggling deviated from that of the West. Between 1949 and 1976, when the market was regulated by the government, *zousi* (smuggling) was simply taking products from one city, region, or province to another without official authorization. In the eighties, the government deregulated state control of a large number of products and smuggling in China began to look more like that in the West. Television sets, stereos, even cars, were transported across the national borders and distributed throughout the country without state authorization and payment of the required taxes.

In the West, state officials involved in smuggling and speculation would most likely be charged for not paying import taxes or dismissed for their participation in "outside" activities; Chinese state officials, in contrast, would be punished for participating in otherwise state-controlled activities—trade and the movement of goods than are organized by the government. Because state officials (more than private citizens) are privy to information on the distribution of goods and they have easy access to the materials, capital, and transportation facilities needed for smuggling and speculation, they are more likely to defy state regulations to enrich themselves. Moreover, these two crimes often go together because the easiest and most common way to make a profit (speculation) is to transport goods from an area where the prices are low and sell them at another where they are high (i.e., smuggling).

Forms of Corruption in Administrative Regulations

The administrative regulations do not necessarily use the same legal jargon as government legislations; the term *tanwu* is used loosely, but the actions being condemned overlap. The October 23, 1957, Regulations on Reward and Punishment of State Administrative Personnel warned state personnel not to indulge in activities that undermined the efficacy of the bureaucracy, such as *tanwu* (corruption). They were cautioned against false reporting and lying to their superiors (regulation 4), embezzlement and theft of state property (regulation 7), and misuse of power and infringement on people's interests (regulation 9). The actions covered by regulation 4 were similar to fraud even though individuals might not get something substantive for their personal use—in the socialist system, many officials submitted false reports so as to remain in the good books of the supervisors. While regulation 7 referred to embezzlement and theft, regulation 9 referred to extortion, appropriation, and seizure of personal properties. Speculation and smuggling were omitted probably because by the mid-fifties such activities had declined with the tighter state control of the market. Almost thirty years later, the State Council's 1982 Work Regulations incorporated similar examples of proscribed behavior. The 1988 Provisional Regulations on the Penalties for Corruption and Bribery of State Administrative Personnel focused on state employees' accepting gifts, commissions (kickbacks), and administrative fees or soliciting other forms of income not specified by the state—illicit activities common among state employees of the period.

If some behavior banned by law as corruption is controversial, then the activities proscribed in the administrative codes are even more controversial. The rules of behavior in the administrative documents are more restrictive than those of the legal code passed by the National People's Congress. The administrative codes warned against dereliction of duty, false accusations, shifting blame, living lavishly, and other such activities.[24] Regulation 11 of the 1957 Regulations on Reward and Punishment of State Administrative Personnel, for example, warned the staff not to indulge in corrupt behavior (*fuhua*) that tarnished the country's reputation, such as excessive eating and drinking, gambling, deceit, belief in superstitions, drunkenness, improprieties, womanizing, or anything offensive to public morality.[25] It was important to behave correctly both on and off the job. In the eighties, state employees were reminded to eschew corruption and inappropriate behavior (*bu zheng zhi feng*) which included bureaucratism (acting like a bureaucrat), squandering public money, enjoying special privileges, accepting bribes, using the backdoor (personal contacts), and cliquism.[26] Moreover, they were to help their colleagues to fight these temptations as well.

Even if we restrict our attention to behavior on the job, some of the activities forbidden in the organizational codes fall into the gray areas of the law. The criminal justice system prosecuted state employees who converted state property into private possessions for corruption. Those who did not do so technically would not be breaking the law even though their actions contravened the spirit of the law to safeguard private and public property. As private ownership was banned in the socialist economy, officials saw little personal advantage in pocketing state property. Instead, they used state resources accessible to them for their own pleasure. They gave lavish banquets on official occasions, eating and drinking on state accounts, and built luxurious offices and spacious official residences for themselves and their staffs—all decisions within their prerogatives. The 1957 Decisions on the Handling of Corruption, Waste, and Bureaucracy were aimed at this problem and labeled the use of public funds to support such actions as *fuhua* (corrupt lifestyle) and *tanwu* (corruption). Work regulations of the seventies and eighties also took a similar stand and disciplined members who ate and drank excessively (*da qi da ke*) at public expense.

The administrative codes broaden the parameters of corruption in another way. Although corruption is legally a property crime, more often than not, officials traded not material property but conveniences, services, and opportunities that could give the recipients great future benefits. These deals might or might not have carried tangible monetary values—for example, negotiating entry into a good school so as to open up new opportunities. Again such a misdemeanor contravened the spirit but not the word of the law. Even in the undeveloped and unsophisticated Chinese court system, prosecutors pursued only cases in which laws were clearly broken and could not bring charges on such thin legal grounds. Nevertheless, the repeated warnings from state organizations on these matters suggest such abuses were not uncommon, and the explicit administrative statements condemning such behavior made it clear that such actions would be not be tolerated.

Even when property was involved, Chinese courts, like those in the West, would not prosecute all the cases brought before them, but pursued only those involving a certain sum of money. The 1952 statute on corruption set a ten-million-yuan minimum, while the 1979 criminal code set it at two thousand yuan, with the amount adjusted upward in later years. The 1952 limit did not represent greater government tolerance of corruption, but rather the effects of inflation, which was rampant in the early fifties—ten thousand yuan was worth only one yuan after the currency reform of 1955.[27] In any event, these limits meant that any corruption cases involving sums below the minimum would be thrown out of court, but no sum was too small for organizational discipline.

Much of the behavior banned in the administrative codes falls into the area of gray corruption in another way. Not only would the courts fail to prosecute state employees for womanizing, banqueting, minor misappropriation of public property or nepotism; the public generally would tolerate limited forms of these behavior. The public condemned nepotism, but personal relationships were deemed important in the particularistic Chinese culture, and people were expected to do favors for family and friends. State employees who turned down such requests might be praised by some as upright officials, but might be considered inflexible and unreasonable by others. Moreover, in the hierarchical nature of traditional Chinese society those at the top were entitled to more privileges than those below. Sybaritic practices among officials were often overlooked as perks that came with these positions so long as these were not excessive—again a matter of personal opinion. This ambiguity, inconsistency and lack of consensus in public opinion as well as the incongruity between official and public perceptions, as we shall see later, undermine the effectiveness of administrative regulations fostering honest governance.

Each organization's rules were specific in their lists of proscribed behavior. For example, court employees were not allowed to let nepotism or personal ties influence their decisions, accept or solicit bribes, be involved in business, or steal public property. Members of investigating teams were not permitted to live in luxury hotels nor to accept food and drink, or gifts and souvenirs, on their tours of duty. In addition, they were not to buy goods that were in short supply or at a discount from clients because such purchases could compromise their judgments.[28] Auditors were to decline invitations to parties and were not to obtain consumer goods at below market price. They were not to take bribes, allow personal connections to influence their work, or misuse their power in any way.[29] In short, in these organizations, indulging in such banned behavior constituted corruption because it meant that these officials were using opportunities afforded by their work situations to benefit themselves.

Chinese state and collective organizations can react more quickly than can the legal system to block ingenious and devious state employees from taking advantage of administrative oversights or omissions. Because administrative regulations are organizational decisions and, as such, are exempted from the laborious vetting and delays that accompany the passing of laws, they can plug loopholes with greater speed. Swift administrative response became especially necessary during the rapid changes of the eighties, which introduced new opportunities for corruption unanticipated by the organization. Bureaucratic regulations proliferated. With each new administrative ruling, behavior once permitted becomes proscribed and subject to discipline. Those who were formerly "smart" could now find themselves "wrong."

A few examples would be appropriate here. In the more liberal climate of the eighties, units produced goods outside the state plan and even ran businesses. Cadres well-positioned in these organizations did the same. In 1984, the State Council forbade the latter practice; in 1985, even cadre children were prohibited from engaging in business. These directives were ignored, but their existence undermined the moral positions and legitimacy of cadres who indulged in these activities. To take another example, it was common for enterprises to provide lunches, clothing, and other consumer items to their staffs from their reserve funds. In 1984, the State Council banned the distribution of clothing; in 1985, organizations were no longer permitted to provide lunches and consumer goods to their personnel. Furthermore, they were warned not to use festive occasions or lotteries to distribute such benefits. Administrators who continued these practices would be considered in the wrong, even though they were not benefiting themselves but their organizational members—an issue to be discussed in the next section.

Although the meaning of corruption, as officials using their position to benefit themselves, has not changed in the forty years between 1949 and 1989, the specific behavior labeled as corruption in both the legal and administrative documents did change. Thus, with the introduction of each new legal or organizational rule, the definition of corruption was altered and the parameters of acceptable or unacceptable behavior changed accordingly.

Individual and Organizational Corruption

Acts of corruption are committed by individuals for personal gain, but the benefits can go to the perpetrators alone, to their families and friends, or be divided among members of their unit. The first instance would be an individual crime; the latter, a corporate or organizational crime. As early as 1952, the administrative document, Decision on the Handling of Corruption, Waste, and Bureaucratism, separated the two. The legal system, however, made no distinction until its Supplementary Regulations Relating to Corruption (*tanwu*) and Bribery in 1988. It distinguished crimes that benefited individuals from those benefiting the "collective unit, the factory, or enterprise" where the benefits were divided among the members, and made the top administrators responsible for such actions.

The meaning of individual crime, where only the individual benefits, is obvious; the other categories, however, deserve some elaboration. The legal codes had always ignored beneficiaries who were neither the actual perpetrators nor fellow members of organizations. The administrative codes, however, repeatedly warned officials not to compromise their principles at work for the benefit of their immediate family members, relatives, or friends. Nepotism is common in China. Chinese culture is particularistic, with the family as the nucleus of one's existence, and ties to kin and friends are intense. The popular attitude toward nepotism is ambivalent. On the one hand, nepotism is condemned; on the other, officials who disregard family interests to adhere strictly to official rules may be accused of being unreasonable or *meiyou renqing wei* (lacking human feelings). State employees often feel such strong obligations toward members of their social network that they would bend rules to meet their needs. Some might give away state property, but more often they provided conveniences, opportunities, or favors whose monetary value is difficult to assess. Furthermore, unlike bribery where clients pay for favors, these beneficiaries often gave nothing more material in return than perhaps gratitude.

In organizational crimes, Chinese state employees acted to benefit their employment units by misrepresenting their products, or by over- or underreporting their performances or needs, as the circumstances dictated. They inflated production figures to get official recognition or underreported their assets to get central government subsidies. The official press condemned such actions as *shantou zhuyi* (mountainism), *benweizhuyi* (departmentalism), or *difang zhuyi* (parochialism), that is, officials put the interests of the small collective (the organization or locality) ahead of those of the larger collective (society). Although the small collective benefited, the larger one usually lost out. For example, if one factory received more materials than it needed by inflating its needs, it deprived another of using the same resources.

The formula for dividing the spoils from such illegal activities seemed to be egalitarian. In the corporate crimes committed in the West, owners and top management are the main beneficiaries, with the rewards usually concentrated at the top. Leaders of organizations in China also had more to gain than the workers in terms of money, reputation, goodwill or the favorable notice of their superiors. But in the collective spirit of Chinese socialism in the fifties and sixties, the organizations as a whole wallowed in the honor of being the first to fulfill their production or work quotas; in the eighties, individual members of the unit stood to benefit from the profits distributed as bonuses or as consumer items.

Definition of Corruption

The legal and administrative codes issued in China between 1949 and 1989 do not offer identical definitions of corruption even in this putatively monolithic country; furthermore, the interpretations offered in both the administrative and legal documents vary over time. They differ in their definitions of who might be the criminals, the nature and value of the "properties" involved, who might be the beneficiaries, and the limits of acceptable behavior. The behavior identified in the legal interpretation falls into what social scientists would consider "black" or clearcut cases of corruption, while the behavior proscribed in the administrative documents falls into the area of "gray" or "white" corruption, that is, the murky areas where there is less consensus.[30]

The 1952 statute treated corruption as a legal category that included theft, bribery, fraud, smuggling, speculation, and other means used by state officials to take over public and private properties. In the related legal documents, such actions were seen as undermining collective well-being and as pertaining to wastefulness and bureaucratism. The 1979 criminal code patterned after those of the West was free of such moralizing. It no longer treated corruption as a legal category but focused instead on behavioral manifestations that could be authenticated in the courts of law and criminalized only specific acts that damaged public or private property. *Tanwu* in 1979 referred simply to the embezzling of state property by state officials, and the other crimes listed in the 1952 statute fell under the sections on property crimes or dereliction of duties governing the behavior of all Chinese citizens.

Corruption in the administrative context touched almost every aspect of state and collective employees' behavior, such as womanizing or drunkenness. Even if one uses the parameters set by the more restrictive 1952 legal interpretation of corruption as the arrogation of public and private property, the administrative meaning of the term is still more comprehensive than the legal one. It went beyond the abuse of ownership rights to incorporate abuses of users' rights. It included, besides privatizing another's property, the misuse of public property and the trading of opportunities, conveniences, and favors. Unlike the legal system, which put a minimum monetary limit on the cases it would prosecute, no amount was too small for the administrative authorities. The legal system was silent on organizational corruption until 1988, but the state administration, as early as 1952, condemned officials who compromised in the performance of their duties to benefit their friends, families and members of the organizations. Given the varied nature of government organs, the opportunities available and the means used to acquire personal gains differed in different governments units. Each department had its set of regulations catering to its special needs; it anticipated the opportunities for abuse and laid out clear interdictions to prohibit unacceptable behavior. While the legal documents were sparse on specifics and the meaning of *tanwu* became more restrictive over time, the meaning of corruption in the administrative codes remained relatively consistent and was steadily informed by the proliferation of organizational rules in the eighties.

Despite these contextual and temporal variations in the interpretation of the term corruption, there are no basic contradictory interpretations to the concept. The specific corrupt actions highlighted in these documents might vary but the essence of the meaning of corruption remains the same—it is the trading of the power vested in one's public office for personal gains. Incumbents break laws or work rules by using the authority, or other resources offered by their positions to deal in public or private property or solicit opportunities to enhance their personal gains.

In the following analysis, I shall adopt a conservative approach and, significantly, also a broader one that incorporates the meanings of corruption from both the legal and administrative codes. For my purposes, the term corruption refers to the breaking of legal or organizational rules by state (and collective) officials at the administrative level so as to misuse, trade, or appropriate material and nonmaterial state and private resources to benefit themselves, their family members and friends, or their organizations. This broad definition, using the limits circumscribed by the administrative and legal codes, incorporates a wide range of actions proscribed in Chinese society, but which may be tolerated in other societies. It also provides a richer texture in which to reflect on the specificities of the historical and social context than would a purely legalistic interpretation.

Notes

1. Thomas A. Metzger, *The Internal Organization of Ch'ing Bureaucracy* (Cambridge, Mass.: Harvard University Press, 1973), pp. 263, 325.
2. For changes in the meaning of corruption in China, see Lynn T. White, "Changing Conceptions of Corruption in Communist China: Early 1950s versus early 1980s," in *Change and Continuities in Chinese Communism*, vol. 2, ed. Yu-ming Shaw, ed. (Boulder: Westview Press, 1988), pp. 316–53.
3. "Corruption and Reform: An Editorial Essay," *Corruption and Reform* 1 (1986): 3–11.
4. *Statistical Yearbook of China, 1991* (Beijing: Zhongguo Tongii Chubanshe, 1991), p. 32.
5. For example, the "Directive on Increasing Production and Eliminating Waste and Fighting Against Corruption, Waste, and Bureaucratism" (December 29, 1951) and the "Decision on the Handling of Corruption, Waste, and Bureaucratism" (March 8, 1952). Bureaucratism refers to following rules and regulations with complete disregard for local needs and conditions.
6. Byron S.J. Weng and Hsin Chang, *Introduction to Chinese Law* (Hong Kong: Ming Pao Publishing, 1988), pp. 230–31.
7. Zhang Huangguang et al., *Zhonghua Renmin Gongheguo Xin Zheng Fa Zi Liao Xuanbian* (Selections of administrative laws in the People's Republic of China) (Beijing: Qunzhong Chubanshe, 1984), p. 661.
8. *Lianzheng Jianshe Shouce* (Handbook to build a clean government), (Chengdu: Sichuan Renmin Chubanshe, 1989), pp. 49–51.
9. Stephen Uhalley, Jr., *A History of the Chinese Communist Party* (Stanford: Stanford University, Hoover Institute, 1988), pp. 155–56, 173–74, 188, 195, 199, 204–5. 242–43.

10. *Renmin Ribao,* September 30, 1952, quoted in Chen Nai-chao, *Zhonggong Tanwu Jiantao* (An examination of corruption in Communist China) (Hong Kong: Xin Shiji Chubanshe, 1953), p. 105, reported 2.74 million working in government departments, and the *Zhongguo Tongji Nianjian, 1991* (p. 95) reported 16.03 million working in nationalized industries in the same year. In 1958, the number in the latter category increased to 57.94 million (ibid.).

11. *The Criminal Law and the Criminal Procedure Law of the People's Republic of China* (Peking: Foreign Languages Press, 1984), p. 33.

12. *Statistical Yearbook of China, 1991,* pp. 97, 107.

13. Most political scientists studying corruption in China, for example, Clemens Stubbe Ostergaard (1986) and Alan P.L. Liu (1983), label it political corruption even when these state appointees, more often than not, are attached to the economic branches and are involved in economic crimes. Peter Nan-shong Lee in "Bureaucratic Corruption During the Deng Xiaoping Era," *Corruption and Reform* 5 (1990):29–47, however, makes the distinction between bureaucratic and political corruption.

14. Yanjie Bian, *Work and Inequality in Urban China.* Albany, N.Y.: State University of New York Press, 1994, pp. 24–38.

15. Wang Juofu, *Zhongguo Falu Yanjiu* (Chinese law research) (Beijing: Zhongguo Renmin Daxue Chubanshe, 1988), p. 624.

16. Huang Shu-min, *The Spiral Road: Changes in a Chinese Village Through the Eyes of a Communist Party Leader* (Boulder: Westview Press, 1989), pp. 163–65.

17. The Chinese government introduced company law, or *gongsi fa,* only in 1994 to protect private owners from dishonest employees embezzling their property.

18. Chao Zhi, ed., *An Outline of the Personnel System in the PRC* (Beijing: Beijing University Press, 1985), p. 258, quoted in Gong Ting, *The Politics of Corruption in Contemporary China: An Analysis of Policy Outcomes* (Westport, Conn.: Praeger, 1994), p. 85.

19. Andrew G. Walder, "Career Mobility and the Communist Political Order" *American Sociological Review* 60 (June 1995): 309–28.

20. *Criminal Law and Criminal Procedure Law,* p. 53.

21. This definition is taken from James C. Scott, "Political Clientelism: A Bibliographic Essay," in *Friends, Followers, and Factions: A Reader in Political Clientelism,* ed. Steffen W. Schmidt, Laura Guasti, Carl H. Lande, and James C. Scott, pp. 483–505 (Berkeley: University of California Press, 1977). It overlaps with J.S. Nye's definition in "Corruption and Political Development: A Cost-Benefit Analysis," *American Political Science Review* 61, no. 2 (June 1967):426, in which he defines corruption as behavior "deviating from the formal duties of a public role (elective or appointive) because of private-regarding (personal, family or clique) wealth or status gains; or violates rules against the exercise of certain types of private-regarding influence." A.J. Heidenheimer, "The Context of Analysis," in *Political Corruption: Readings in Comparative Analysis,* ed. A.J. Heidenheimer, p. 5 (New Brunswick, N.J.: Transaction Books, 1978) defines corruption as a "general term covering misuse of authority as a result of consideration of personal gain, which need not be monetary."

22. In the Confucian social order, the ranks are scholars, peasants, workers, and traders. See Dorothy J. Solinger, *Chinese Business Under Socialism: The Politics of Domestic Commerce, 1949–1980* (Berkeley: University of California Press, 1984), pp. 30–31, for a discussion of the market in Marxism.

23. Henry Campbell Black, *Black's Law Dictionary* (St. Paul, Minn.: West Publishing, 1979).

24. Gong Ting, *Politics of Corruption,* p. 9.

25. Li Zhisui, *The Private Life of Chairman Mao* (New York: Random House, 1994), for example, considers Mao's womanizing and his entourage's indulgence in food as corrupt.

26. *Renmin Ribao,* July 1, 1979.

27. Tadao Miyashita, *The Currency and Financial System of Mainland China* (Seattle: University of Washington Press, 1966), pp. 68, 81. The exchange rate was officially pegged at 2.46 yuan to U.S.$1.00 in 1952 and 1955 [Alexander Eckstein, *China's Economic Development: The Interplay of Scarcity and Ideology* (Ann Arbor: University of Michigan Press, 1985), p. 42; *International Monetary Fund, International Financial Statistics* (Washington, D.C.: International Monetary Fund, February 1955), p. 15]. The rate did not reflect the devaluation of the yuan inside the country.

28. *Renmin Ribao,* December 19, 1987, p. 1.

29. *Renmin Ribao,* July 23, 1988, p. 1.

30. Heidenheimer, *Political Corruption,* pp. 3–28.

2

Social Context

The Chinese interpretation of corruption overlaps the generally accepted one in the West. It condemns the use of public office for personal gains, and yet it has its distinctive meaning. The Chinese are at once more tolerant of some forms of corruption and less of others. State employees in China can divert public funds for personal use for a limited time, while such action by civil servants in the West would be prosecuted for embezzlement. Western civil servants can engage in business so long as such outside engagements are not prohibited by the employers and so long as these activities do not interfere with their official roles, but for more than thirty years in China they would be criticized for speculation and exhibiting the "tails (signs) of capitalism." Chinese officials who improve state employees' working or living conditions may be criticized for extravagance; while the same action in privately owned industries in the West is seen as employers' taking care of workers. In capitalist societies, a company's entertainment budget is of little interest to the government except for tax purposes, and more often than not commissions on sales constitute an integral part of the salespersons' legitimate income. Under the Chinese socialist system, however, these actions come under close government scrutiny because they are outlawed.

These differences in proscribing and criminalizing behavior reflect the particular moral and political standpoints of capitalist and socialist societies as well as their different social realities. The actions proscribed by the Chinese legal and administrative codes are not mere congeries of the policymakers' imagination or viewpoints, or simply articulations of the larger culture, but reflect the social structures as well as the ways dishonest civil servants commonly used to benefit themselves. Since the shaping of positions, definitions of reality, and behavior of individuals depend on the organization of the society, the political economy of Chinese socialism in these forty years deserves closer scrutiny.

Socialist China

In Marx's writings, socialism is a transition bridging the stages of capitalism and communism.[1] Communism, the last stage of social development, produces the utopian society in which government has become obsolete, members contribute according to their ability, and goods are distributed to those in need. In contrast, capitalism is characterized by exploitation and inequities. State power is in the hands of the bourgeoisie, and workers expend their energy and resources only to be given subsistence wages. A socialist society moving from capitalism to communism shares features common to both systems.

Lenin elaborated on the characteristics of the socialist state.[2] In this transitional period, dictatorship of the proletariat replaces the domination of the capitalists. Unlike the Communist utopia in which the state disappears, government here is an instrument to protect proletarian interests and curtail capitalist influences. Furthermore, to safeguard against the threat of capitalist conspiracy and revival, power has to be concentrated in the government under the direction and supervision of the Communist Party, the vanguard of the proletariat.

In the Marxist view, the economy is the foundation that gives shape to the sociopolitical superstructure of a society. Therefore, the first task of any socialist government is to transform the nature of the economic substructure. The first item of a socialist economic program is usually the confiscation of foreign investments and large holdings, followed by the division of private property among the general population, and the strict regulation of the operations of industry and agriculture. The ideal socialist society enjoys nationalized industry and agriculture, central planning of the economy, and state control of production. These measures of tight control are to forestall the manipulation of the market by the capitalists, and thus to ensure full employment, a steady supply of goods and a more equitable distribution of rewards to the population.

Contemporary China qualifies as a socialist society because the Communist Party, the self-proclaimed party of the proletariat, controls state governance. The party expounds and propagates the Communist ideology of Marxism-Leninism, and directs and supervises an authoritarian state structure. More importantly, private ownership of the means of production has been abolished. Even in the last decade, when a more liberal economic policy has been pursued, only the leasing of land is permitted—outright ownership is banned. Foreign ownership is safeguarded by joint ventures, and privatization of large enterprises is forestalled with government owning half of the shares. The major industries are state- or collectively owned, and their operations are under strict government plan and supervision, with the free market playing a limited role.

Although socialism was the foundation for Chinese development over these forty years (1949–1989), to characterize the society simply as socialist denies both the subtle and traumatic changes it experienced. The different emphases given to the meaning of corruption in the legal sense, as described in chapter 1, suggest something less than a gradual or homogeneous evolution. In the earlier period, corruption is framed in a broad moralistic and developmental perspective, while in the seventies it is given a narrower and more bureaucratic meaning. Such variations cannot but reflect at the very least some fundamental changes in the political economy within the socialist framework, such as the evolution from a broad moralistic to a technocratic ethos.

Sinologists, with some exceptions, have generally viewed recent Chinese history as the swinging of the pendulum between the developmental model of Mao Zedong, on one side, and that of Liu Shaoqi/Deng Xiaoping, on the other. The former opted for strategies that followed more closely the Marxist blueprint; the latter has preferred a pragmatic approach, relying on material incentives and the market. Behind these policy shifts is a continuous power struggle between factions with different philosophies, prognoses of the situation, priorities, and management styles. When the rivalry between Mao and Liu/Deng dominated the political arena, the composition of their supporters differed in the different periods and the actors in these alliances sometimes changed camps.[3]

Chinese socialism has followed Janos Kornai's historical prototypes: the revolutionary transition period, the classical socialist period, and the reform socialist period.[4] The transitional period, however, was short; the Communist Party consolidated its hold in less than three years. Because of its brevity, I have incorporated this phase into the second period, classical socialism, and divided the forty years into two broad periods—recognizing that ideological and policy fluctuations occurred within each era.

The classical socialist period extends from the assumption of power by the Communists in 1949 to the death of Mao in September 1976. These years mark the deliberate attempts by the political leaders to dismantle the Guomindang political economy and establish a Communist one. Private ownership was abolished, industry and agriculture were nationalized, and their operations came under state control. The next period, reform socialism, began with Mao's death and lasted until May 1989, when students demonstrated against government corruption on Tian'anmen Square. In order to revitalize a sagging economy, the political leaders abandoned the dogmatic socialist approach and reversed some earlier economic policies. They reintroduced the market, limited forms of ownership, and greater individual initiatives in production. Nevertheless they left state ownership and central planning of the major industries intact, kept Marxism-Leninism as the state ideology, and preserved the Communist Party's dominance in governance.

Classical Socialism, 1949–1976

The Communists declared the formation of the People's Republic of China in October 1949, but their control of the country was far from complete. Military control was confined to the northeast; they did not occupy the west and southwest until 1951.[5] But in the initial years, their political hold within the occupied regions was tenuous. Communist ideology was very different from that of the Guomindang, which it replaced, and from that of the population at large. The Chinese populace was apolitical. Few knew what communism was and, if they did, would probably disagree with its major tenets of public ownership and planned economy. The Chinese peasantry, which constituted more than 90 percent of the population, would prefer their private plots of land. Even among the highly politicized student body in Beijing, only 50 percent knew anything of or were sympathetic to communism.[6] The majority of the population was tired of the turmoil in the last fifty years. They saw the Communist Party as providing a more honest government compared with the Guomindang, an alternative that might give the people peace and allow the country to recuperate. In a sense, the Communist Party was on political probation.

Under the Communists, the country was divided into six administrative military regions.[7] At the center was the People's Government Council—the most powerful political organ. It consisted of party faithful exercising legislative and executive power by formulating policies, directing the activities of all government organs, controlling the budget and state accounting, and appointing all key government personnel. Under the People's Government Council were the four executive branches: the Government Administrative Council, the People's Revolutionary Military Council, the Supreme People's Court, and the People's Procurator-General's Office.* The Administrative Council was the most important branch as it was concerned with political and administrative affairs, finance and economics, culture and education, and staff supervision.

This early military administrative structure was replaced by a

---

*The procurator general carried out functions similar to the attorney general in the West.

civil governing structure when the constitution was ratified in 1954.
The country was divided into twenty-two provinces, special munici-
palities, and autonomous areas. The People's Government Council
was replaced by the People's Congress, and the Government Administrative Council by the State Council, with its subordinate ministries. The number of ministries varied over the next forty years
but the basic political structure of the country remained the same.
Among other important changes, the leadership of the Communist
Party was confirmed in state administration by the constitution
when it declared the party the supreme ruling group in the country
and its ideology the guide for governance.[8]

In the early fifties, civil servants who had worked for the
Guomindang were kept on the government payroll for pragmatic
reasons. There were not enough Communist Party faithful to staff
the government offices. In 1949, the civil service numbered
720,000; by 1952, it had expanded to 2.75 million.[9] There were 4.5
million party members, with over a third joining on the eve of the
Communist victory in 1949.[10] One might suspect the latecomers of
opportunism. Furthermore, party members had been recruited
mainly from the countryside; about 69 percent of its members were
peasants, and 14 percent were workers.[11] Many were illiterate, with
less than 5 percent having received any higher education.[12] Party
members might have been veteran guerilla fighters but they had
little experience in administration. To preserve continuity in governance and to cut down on disruption, often only the heads of the
departments were replaced, while the rank and file were generally
holdovers from the previous administration; some two million
Guomindang functionaries retained their positions.[13] A. Doak Barnett describes the takeover of power in the Bank of China in Beijing
in 1949 as follows:

> There, we had a twenty-minute interview with the man in charge, the
> former deputy manager. After this conversation the Communist said,
> "Let's visit the plant." There he gave the place a quick once-over,
> asked a number of questions about organization, production, meth-
> ods and wages, and then turned to the deputy manager. "You

seemed to know what you've been doing. You're in charge," he said. He handed over the new plates for People's Bank notes and ordered the plant to continue normal operations.[14]

Similar procedures were used in the takeover of the municipal government. Here, Ye Jianying, the new mayor, came in and humbly said that he had a lot to learn from the existing members and invited them to stay.

To prevent sabotage and insubordination, the government adopted the Russian style of one-man management in state administration. This produced a tight organizational structure with a clear chain of command. The central government made decisions, delineated strategies and implementation procedures, and transmitted the information to the lower echelons. Factories, for example, received instruction plans on investment, budget, supplies, production, and distribution. Only one person, the politically dependable head, was in control and made all the decisions. Orders flowed from the top. Work plans were precisely formulated, and job tasks specified in the minutest details. Those below simply followed instructions. The same management style was practiced within each unit down to the lowest level.

After the Communist Party organized a series of ideological campaigns and launched a vigorous recruitment program to consolidate their ranks, membership rose from 4.5 million in 1949 to 6.5 million in 1954 , and to 12.7 million in 1957.[15] As a result, by 1957, party members infiltrated every branch and every level of state governance; the party organization formed an administrative channel parallel to that of the state. According to the constitution, the party provided directions to state administration and supervised state operations; the state administration looked after everyday matters of governance. In practice, this division of labor was blurred, with the party intervening in and often superseding the authority of state governance. The chain of command emanating from the state council, and a parallel one originating in the central committee of the party reaching down to the grass roots, produced a network of tight control over the Chinese civil service.

When the state administration scrutinized employees in the discharge of their official duties, the party also monitored every aspect of their behavior.

True, the Chinese bureaucracies went through periods of centralization and decentralization. But, as both Nicholas Lardy and Carl Riskin have pointed out, decentralization in the late fifties meant greater financial autonomy for the provinces vis-à-vis the center, or the enterprises versus the ministries, but not greater autonomy for the staff working in the bureaucracy.[16] Directives continued to come from immediate superiors, and their subordinates fulfilled the assigned tasks. Meetings were held to discuss central policies, but they were not opportunities to elicit genuine debate, rather they served the pedagogical purpose of familiarizing the members with government intentions.

The party and state administrations were dismantled in the heady days of the Cultural Revolution (1966–1976) and replaced by revolutionary committees made up of representatives of the proletariat —industrial workers, peasants, and soldiers. The party structure was revived in 1969, but its prestige was severely tarnished in the turmoils of the mass movement of the last three years. Nevertheless, the monolithic chain of command, or what the Chinese called *yiyuanhua lingdao,* and the hold of the organization on the members persisted. The central revolutionary committee, with its lower echelons of revolutionary committees, penetrated the grass roots. Party members again controlled the revolutionary committees, but the new incumbents, of course, owed their allegiance to the new leaders now dominating the central revolutionary committee.

Because of political weakness in the early fifties, the government proceeded cautiously with its economic programs, shelving the more radical socialist policies such as public ownership and focusing instead on restoring economic stability. In addition to nationalizing foreign assets, the government appropriated only strategic essential industries, such as banking, transportation, iron, and steel. Former owners received interest from their investment in these enterprises and were encouraged to remain as managers and consultants.

Nevertheless, the trend toward increased state control of the economy was obvious. In 1949, the private sector contributed 72 percent of the gross industrial output, and the state enterprises, 26 percent. By 1954, the positions were reversed—returns from the private sector dropped to 38 percent and those from the public sector rose to 47 percent.[17] Similar developments could also be seen in the employment pattern. In 1949, about 53 percent of the three million industrial workers were employed in private enterprises; by 1955, their numbers had declined to less than 22 percent of the industrial labor force, which had almost doubled in size.[18] In finance, private banks were allowed to operate, but were increasingly edged out as more and more industries came under state control and deposits went to the government-run Bank of China. By 1955, state-owned enterprises accounted for 68 percent of the gross value of industrial output; joint private-state ventures, 16 percent; and private companies executing state orders, 13 percent. Only 3 percent of business came from truly privately owned and operated firms.[19]

Under strong political pressure even owners of joint enterprises petitioned in 1956 to turn their businesses into state ones, and private operation of firms involved in industry, commerce, transportation, and services was eliminated. From then until 1966, one million former owners received close to 5 percent interest per annum on the assessed value of their shares. At about the same time, artisans were organized into cooperatives or were lured into jobs in state factories.[20]

The role of the market weakened tremendously. The government regulated the distribution of goods, and essential commodities, such as grain and cotton, came under price control. In 1952, the prices of twenty-eight items were regulated, and inflation was reduced to less than 20 percent. In 1953, the list increased to ninety-six items,[21] and the overall rise in prices came to a virtual halt.[22] Encouraged by this success, state intervention in the market escalated, and commerce almost disappeared. By 1956, 235 items were state regulated and consumer prices on goods varied only slightly across the nation.[23] State trading companies replaced private wholesalers and retailers in the distribution of consumer goods, and regulated the needs of supply and demand among the populace based on information or estimates provided by economic units across the country. The state distribution system was in place.

The June 28, 1950, Agrarian Reform Law unleashed a massive rural campaign affecting all Chinese agriculture. About three hundred million peasants joined peasant's associations, denounced feudal exploitation, criticized the landlords, and divided approximately forty-six million hectares, or half the country's cultivated land, among themselves.[24] In 1951, some peasant households engaged in cooperative production on a seasonal basis. By 1952, about 40 percent of farm families had formed mutual aid teams working year-round on their private plots with pooled resources of labor and implements. At the same time, some teams had evolved into agricultural cooperatives in which twenty to thirty households collectively owned the implements and the land, and members were paid for their work and investments from sales of produce.[25] By 1954, 120 million, or 11 percent, of the agricultural households belonged to 740,000 such cooperatives.[26]

With their hold on the bureaucracy consolidated, political leaders abandoned the gradual approach of the early fifties. On July 31, 1955, Mao issued the directive on collective transformation in agriculture and exerted strong pressure on officials to implement the policy; rural cadres in turn coerced the peasants. Within six months, mutual aid teams virtually disappeared and the number of households belonging to agriculture cooperatives jumped from only 14 percent in June to 63 percent in December 1955. A year later, over 96 percent of the rural households belonged to cooperatives.[27]

Confidence came with success. Collectivization of agriculture escalated during 1958–1959, known as the Great Leap Forward. The Beidaihe guidelines issued in August 1958 replaced the township, or *xiang*, with communes as the basic political unit in rural China. In addition to their political responsibilities, commune cadres took on such economic duties as formulating production plans, providing inputs, collecting taxes and grain procurements for the state, and distributing the surplus. Below the communes were production brigades (comparable to the village) and production teams.

The production teams were the basic work unit and coordinated production activities, such as scheduling, methods of sowing, fertilizing, harvesting, and irrigation, among thirty- to forty-member households. Four months after the publication of the Beidaihe guidelines, over 120 million households belonging to 740,000 collectives were reorganized into 26,000 communes; these remained the basic structural units of rural China until they were dismantled in 1984.[28]

As a result of these changes, the state and the Communist Party controlled not only political governance, economic planning, and distribution of resources at the macro level but also the individual at the micro level. The hold of the work organization (including the production team in the rural areas) on the individual in China was encompassing and strong. At the height of the Great Leap Forward in 1958, work units even provided communal eating and childcare services. Although such extreme forms of state services were abandoned within a few months, work units continued to give members employment and income, and also amenities covering almost every aspect of a person's life, including housing, eating facilities, health care for the employee and the family, and education for the children. Individuals were dependent on their employers, there were few or no legitimate sources outside the work unit for satisfying these needs. Furthermore, after the rectification campaign of 1957, the work units took over the largely defunct criminal justice system so that during the classical socialist period, the work units dispensed not only material goods but justice as well. They enveloped a person's existence. In a highly centralized society where the state was the only employer and jobs lasted a lifetime, individuals could find no exit or escape from such control. The power of the top administrators was supreme.

Reform Socialism, 1976–1989

Unlike in Eastern Europe, the transition from classical to reform socialism in China was gradual and unaccompanied by blueprints or dramatic pronouncements. By the mid-seventies, the majority of the population had forgotten or had never experienced the wars and ravages of the Republican or Guomindang period. Instead, they were confused and tired of the continuous political campaigns of the Cultural Revolution and wanted only "peace." The population was freed from the vagaries of the pre-liberation period. Their basic needs were satisfied, but the standard of living was not high. Some were dissatisfied with their living conditions and the constant appeal from the party to sacrifice for the future. The utopia promised by communism seemed far off. These sentiments were echoed by the opposition at the center. Many leaders had suffered from the purges of the previous decades. They resented the political approach of Maoist economic strategy and were impatient with the slow economic progress. Moreover, they were troubled by the lack of motivation for work among the populace. With this resonance between the grass roots and some leaders, China was ready for change.

The death of Mao Zedong on September 26, 1976, provided the opportunity. Without Mao's backing, the Gang of Four lost the struggle for power. Hua Guofeng, Mao's appointed successor, abandoned the Gang's autarkic orientation, initiated trade with the West, and imported foreign technology. Hua's program, however, remained too Maoist to satisfy the opposition, and in 1980 he too was ousted when his economic measures produced a hefty national deficit. Deng Xiaoping took over control. In 1978, he supported Zhao Ziyang's relaxed and decentralized economic policies in Sichuan and Wan Li's more daring agricultural programs in Anhui, which entailed the devolution of farming responsibilities to the households. Other parts of the country were encouraged to emulate these examples, modifying the policies to fit their respective needs. Soon variants of the "responsibility system" were introduced nationally into agriculture, industry, and even government administration.

The new measures were adopted in an effort to increase output. The reformers felt that tight bureaucratic control was stifling the economy. If basic production units were given more freedom in making plans and carrying them out, they would take greater initiative and utilize idle local resources to manufacture goods needed by the consumers. The potentials for further development were there; but the availability of hidden resources and information on possible markets were known only by those at the local level. To encourage these units to make the extra efforts, the government would allow them to keep part of the profits from such endeavors. Material incentives also were used within the work units to improve performance by tying a worker's income more closely to individual efforts and giving bonuses to those who produced above the designated amount.

Profit motivation and material incentives would have been anathema to the pristine socialist ideology of the earlier period, but, in Deng's pragmatic view, such deviations did not matter, it was the result that counted—"It does not matter whether a cat is black or white, so long as it catches mice." This pragmatic outlook affected the official conception of corruption as well. Unlike the administrative documents of the earlier period, directives on corruption in this period were stripped of ideological overtones, such as serving the collective. Both the legal and administrative documents dealing with corruption moved from a broad inclusive orientation to a focus on concrete behavioral manifestations among state employees.

The responsibility system, which drove the radical transformation of agriculture, underwent a metamorphosis after 1980. In its earlier form, responsibilities were assigned to the *zu,* a smaller unit created below the team level; then, the individual household became the basic production unit. At first, the team supplied inputs, such as land, seeds, fertilizers, and insecticides; in return, the basic production units were to produce a specified amount. Soon, production tools were divided among the households and land was contracted out on a three-to-five-year period. In 1984, the Central Committee's No. 1 Document extended the lease to "no more than 15 years"; by 1988, leases were extended to fifty years in some areas. The distribution of rewards also underwent radical changes. In its initial form, the responsibility system continued to tie household income to the team's collective effort.

Households received bonus work points when they produced above the required quota, but the value of the work points depended on the collective output. Document No. 1 of 1983 and 1984 eliminated this interdependence between private efforts and collective distribution. Households still had to fulfill their sales quotas and tax obligations to the state, but surplus product could be sold to the state at a higher negotiated price or in the newly endorsed free market.

By the end of 1983, over 98 percent of the communes had adopted the new accounting system in which they retained only nominal property ownership rights; the rights to land use had already been given to the households. The central directive of 1984 calling for the separation of economic and political responsibilities of the communes only confirmed a fait accompli. Nevertheless, the dismantling of the commune removed an important cornerstone of Chinese socialism and also the tight control of the government over agricultural production.[29]

As in the transition period, the government acted more cautiously in the industrial sector. Changes of a similar nature were introduced, tying income or profit to performance evaluated in terms of output, quality, and production costs, but these changes did not go as far as those in agriculture. State enterprises remained under national ownership, with the government specifying production line and output quota and providing the inputs; however, state enterprises could also engage in other production plans and ventures. They could seek alternate sources of input, produce beyond the specified state quota, venture into new products, and find markets for their above-quota production. This dual approach of operation not only governed the relationship between state enterprises and those in the higher echelons, but also influenced the relationships within these units. The enterprise could engage in private endeavors; its subunits or departments could do the same. Each level was given a greater degree of fiscal autonomy and could retain a share of their profits. With the introduction of the tax system in 1984, enterprises remitted 55 percent of their profits to the central government and shared the remaining 45 percent with the provinces.[30]

There was some isolated experimentation similar to the more

radical forms of the agricultural responsibility system, in which factories were contracted out to individual managers in return for a specified sum to be paid to the state, with the managers retaining any above-quota-profit. This system, however, was never implemented on a large scale because of the myopic behavior of many contractors who milked the enterprises under their jurisdiction by exhausting the potentials of the plant and leaving the machines in disrepair.

The responsibility system also extended into the social services, military, and administrative departments. To augment their operating budgets, these units were given permission to capitalize on their resources and set up businesses. They too could retain the after-tax profits. In 1989, about seven hundred companies were set up in this way by the ministries and commissions under the State Council.[31] This practice proliferated; but the devolution of fiscal responsibility in government administration was clouded in controversy. Public opinion could not quite accept the fact that social services departments were taking part in business, especially when their preoccupation with business sometimes interfered with their performance or, worse still, when they became involved in shady business practices.

The above-quota goods produced by the agricultural households, industrial enterprises, and government departments needed distribution outlets. Therefore, the state had to provide appropriate channels unless it was ready to buy all the above-quota products. State-controlled markets had always existed, but the exchanges were between government units working under the central plan.[32] Free markets existed on a very small scale in the "private" transactions between government units or in rural areas where peasants sold the produce of their tiny private plots. In the period of reform socialism, consumer markets proliferated. By 1987, there were seventy thousand in the country operating alongside the state markets to form an integral part of the Chinese economy.[33]

Furthermore, the government decontrolled prices of over ten thousand products in 1979 but continued to regulate capital goods, such as iron and steel, used within the planned economy. By 1989, even the proportion of capital goods under state control declined to 20 to 30 percent. To further encourage above quota production, on October 1984 the Central Party Committee issued the directive, "On the Reform of the Economic Structure," which created the triple pricing system. Goods produced beyond the state quota could be sold at higher negotiated prices to the state or traded at a still higher market price.[34]

By the mid-eighties, the more efficient deployment of labor power under the new economic policies had created a pool of surplus labor, more capital for investment, and greater buying power in many rural areas. Encouraged by the government attitude toward entrepreneurship, rural development, and the freedoms accorded to economic units, local governments and state enterprises undertook collective and private initiatives to escape central jurisdiction and appropriation of their profits. The number of rural enterprises jumped from 1.5 million in 1978 to 18 million in 1989, their workforce grew from twenty-eight to almost ninety-four million in the same period,[35] and their output rose from 7 to 33 percent of the value of the nation's total industrial output between 1978 and 1987.[36]

Private enterprises as a proportion of state industries remained small, but they were significant because they represented a different economic form within a socialist economy. In 1982, for the first time in more than twenty-five years, private enterprises appeared as a category in China's economic statistics. In 1985, these 9.3 million private enterprises constituted about 3 percent of the enterprises in the country; by 1988, they rose to 22 million, or 5 percent.[37]

While the Soviet Union focused on political reforms, the Chinese introduced radical economic changes. The leadership still reiterated its adherence to the four basic principles: the socialist road, proletarian dictatorship, the Communist Party, and the ideology of Marxism-Leninism and Mao Zedong Thought. The political structure remained intact. Although freer elections were allowed in the selection of party or some administrative executives, these candidates generally had to be approved by the party. The more important structural reorganization occurred in the economic arena. However, even though production units had additional freedoms in certain areas of operation, they remained under the tight control of the central government, which still handed down production quotas and guaranteed supplies and outlets for their products. At the grass roots, the system of one-man management remained firmly in place, and the heads of the units continued to hold an inordinate amount of power over their staff. According to some sinologists, the additional responsibilities given to the local heads freed them to some degree from central intervention and the increased resources left at their disposal enhanced their power and control over the individuals in the units.[38]

Economic Performance

In the forty years between 1949 and 1989, China existed as a socialist country under the tight political control of the Communist Party. The major means of production were owned by the state or collective. The economy was centrally planned, with the government designating the kinds and quantities of outputs, designing the production process, and organizing the distribution of the goods. This political system seemed to have produced impressive economic results. Except in the early sixties, when the economy suffered from the excesses of the Great Leap Forward, bad harvests, and the sudden withdrawal of Russian aid, and in the late sixties, when production was interrupted by the political turmoil of the Cultural Revolution, the value of economic output rose steadily from 101 billion yuan in 1952 to 543 billion yuan in 1976, and to 2,925 billion yuan in 1988.[39] National income, which is the wealth generated in the production process,* rose more than seven times from 35.8 billion yuan in 1949 to 247.2

---

*National income in China is the value created during production. In line with the Marxist ideology, the Chinese government put great emphasis on the value generated in the production process. The value of national income is obtained by subtracting the cost of production from the total value of national production. The latter includes output in agriculture, industry, construction, transportation, and commerce.

billion yuan in 1976, and quintupled between 1976 and 1989.[40]

Economic growth was especially spectacular in the first five years of Communist rule when national income more than doubled, rising at about 20 percent annually, when grain tonnage increased by 30 percent, and the value of industrial output went up by 50 percent.[41] Although economic growth slowed in the next twenty years, the 1976 grain output was still 55 percent above that of 1955, and the value of industrial output multiplied sixfold, from 53 billion yuan to 328 billion yuan. The growth rate picked up again in the reform socialist period. Between 1976 and 1989, grain output rose by 33 percent, reaching 4,073 billion tons in 1989, and the industrial output multiplied sixfold in the thirteen years, reaching a value of 1,810 billion yuan in 1988.[42]

Under the Communist ideology, any improvement in the economy was ultimately to benefit the population, but the standard of living in China did not keep up with the rate of economic growth. The population was largely relieved from the difficulties of the pre-1949 life and enjoyed a certain degree of financial stability, with the state stepping in to provide the basic social benefits such as housing, health, education, and welfare. But like other socialist countries, China spent an average of 37 percent and 31 percent of its annual budgets on capital investments in the classical socialist period, and the reform socialist period, respectively.[43] With such a heavy commitment of its returns to capital investment, increases in individual income did not keep up with the rate of economic growth.

The average salary rose only from 427 yuan per annum in 1952 to 564 yuan in 1976, an increase of 32 percent—a far cry from the sixfold increase in industrial output. About 60 percent of workers' income was spent on food; in spite of stable market prices, they had little left for other purchases.[44] Some have estimated that the standard of living even declined during the ten years of the Cultural Revolution (1966–1976).[45] Between 1976 and 1989, average individual income more than tripled, rising from 575 yuan to 1,935 yuan.[46] In addition to their salary, many workers received bonuses, subsidies, and overtime pay, which taken together added a substantial proportion to their income. This increase in income during the reform socialist period, however, was to some extent offset by inflation. With the removal of price control on many consumer items, China experienced inflation of 12 percent in 1985, 7 percent in 1986 and 1987, and 18.5 percent in 1988.[47] Furthermore, rural–urban disparity remained with city dwellers earning more than twice the average income of their rural counterparts, and the gap between the rich and the poor regions widened.[48] According to James Ethridge, while income on the whole improved, about 20 percent of the population experienced a loss in income in 1987 and another 35 percent suffered a decline in 1988.[49]

Nonetheless, in the eighties the average Chinese consumer was spending a smaller proportion of his/her income on food, with more money left for other consumer items. During the classical socialist period, with the government investing eight times more in heavy industry than in light industry, there were few goods available and supplies were scarce for the average Chinese consumer.[50] In the period of reform socialism, government priorities shifted slightly toward light industries, and collective and private light industries proliferated at the local level. The number of retail stores jumped from 20 to 102 per ten thousand population between 1980 and 1985, and the merchandise was more varied and plentiful.[51] The number of sewing machines, wrist watches, bicycles, and radios owned by Chinese households jumped fourfold.[52] Televisions, sofas, stereos, washing machines, and refrigerators replaced watches, bicycles, and sewing machines as coveted items and became staples in many homes.[53] By 1989, China's experiment in reform socialism seemed to be succeeding.

Notes

1. Karl Marx, *The Communist Manifesto* (London: Penguin, 1985); *Essential Writings of Karl Marx* (New York: Macmillan, 1987); *Karl Marx: On Society and Social Change* (Chicago: University of Chicago Press, 1973); *Karl Marx: Economy, Class, and Social Revolution* (New York: Scribner 1975).

2. Vladimir Illich Lenin, *State and Revolution* (New York: International Publishers, 1932); *Selected Works* (New York: International Publishers, 1935).

3. Dorothy Solinger, *Chinese Business Under Socialism: The Politics of Domestic Commerce, 1949–1980* (Berkeley: University of California Press, 1984).

4. Janos Kornai, *The Socialist System: The Political Economy of Communism* (Princeton: Princeton University Press, 1992), pp. 19–20.

5. James Pinckney Harrison, *The Long March to Power: A History of the Chinese Communist Party, 1921–1972* (New York: Praeger, 1972), p. 434.

6. A. Doak Barnett, *China on the Eve of Communist Takeover* (New York: Praeger, 1962), p. 46.

7. Carl Riskin, *China's Political Economy: The Quest for Development Since 1949* (Oxford: Oxford University Press, 1987), p. 41.

8. Derek J. Waller, *The Government and Politics of the People's Republic of China* (London: Hutchinson, 1973), p. 97.

9. *Renmin Ribao,* September 30, 1952, in Chen Nai-chao Zhonggong Tanwu Jiantao, *An Examinaton of Corruption in Communist China* (Hong Kong: Xin Shiji Chubanshe 1953), p. 105.

10. Harrison, *Long March,* p. 450.

11. Witold Rodzinski, *The People's Republic of China: A Concise Political History* (New York: Free Press, 1988), p. 47.

12. Harrison, *Long March,* p. 456.

13. Han Suyin, *Eldest Son: Zhou Enlai and the Making of Modern China* (New York: Hull and Wang, 1994), p. 229.

14. Barnett, *China on the Eve,* p.341.

15. Tony Saich, *China: Politics and Government* (New York: St. Martin's Press, 1981), p. 113.

16. Nicholas Lardy, *Economic Growth and Distribution in China* (Cambridge: Cambridge University Press, 1978), p. 33–34; Riskin, *China's Political Economy,* p. 105.

17. *Zhongguo Tongji Nianjian, 1984* (Statistical yearbook of China), Chinese overseas edition (Beijing: People's Republic of China Statistical Bureau, 1984), p. 194.

18. Riskin, *China's Political Economy,* p. 61.

19. *Ten Great Years* (Beijing: Foreign Languages Press, 1960), p. 38.

20. Riskin, *China's Political Economy,* chapter 5.

21. Lardy, *Economic Growth,* p. 15.

22. Riskin, *China's Political Economy,* p. 43.

23. Lardy, *Economic Growth,* p. 15.

24. Rodzinski, *People's Republic,* p. 20.

25. Riskin, *China's Political Economy,* p. 68.

26. *Renmin Ribao,* December 30, 1958, p. 1.

27. See Huang Shu-min, *The Spiral Road: Change in a Chinese Village Through the Eyes of a Communist Party Leader* (Boulder: Westview Press, 1989), chapter 9, on the breakup of the communes in a village in Fujian.

28. Riskin, *China's Political Economy,* chapter 5 and pp. 123–25; *Zhongguo Tongji Nianjian 1981* (Statistical yearbook of China) (Hong Kong: Jingji Daobao

Chubanshe, 1982), p. 131; *Renmin Ribao,* December 30, 1958, p. 1; Xue Muqiao, *China's Socialist Economy* (Beijing: Foreign Languages Press, 1981), p. 35.

29. Thomas Gold, "Still on the Collective Road: Limited Reform in a North China Village," and Jean C. Oi, "The Chinese Village Incorporated," in *Chinese Economic Policy: Economic Reform at Midstream,* ed. Bruce L. Reynolds and Ilpyong J. Kim, pp. 41–66, 67–88 (New York: Paragon House, 1988).

30. Peter Nan-shong Lee, *Industrial Management and Economic Reform in China, 1949–1984* (Oxford: Oxford University Press, 1987), p. 206.

31. *Renmin Ribao,* August 30, 1989, quoted in Gong Ting, *The Politics of Corruption in Contemporary China* (Westport, Conn.: Praeger, 1994), p. 130.

32. Wu Jinglian and Zhao Renwei, "The Dual Pricing System in China's Industry," in *Chinese Economic Reform: How Far, How Fast?* ed. Bruce L. Reynolds, p. 20 (Boston: Academic Press, 1988).

33. James M. Ethridge, *China's Unfinished Revolution: Problems and Prospects Since Mao* (San Francisco: China Books and Periodicals, 1990), p. 167.

34. Wu Jinglian and Zhao Renwei, "Dual Pricing, p. 22; *World Bank, China Between Plan and Market,* (Washington, D.C.: World Bank, 1990), p. 60.

35. *Statistical Yearbook of China, 1991,* p. 377.

36. Ethridge, *Unfinished Revolution,* p. 179.

37. Ibid., pp. 100, 146; Suzanne Ogden, *China's Unresolved Issues: Politics, Development, and Culture* (New York: Prentice Hall, 1989), p. 271.

38. Gong Ting, *Politics of Corruption,* p.125; Vivienne Shue, *The Reach of the State* (Stanford: Stanford University Press, 1988).

39. *Statistical Yearbook of China, 1991,* p. 95.

40. *China's Statistical Abstract, 1989* (New York: Praeger, 1989), p. 89.

41. *Zhongguo Tongji Nianjian, 1984,* p. 29.

42. Ibid., pp. 23, 29, 141, 195; *Zhongguo Tongji Nianjian, 1990* (Statistical yearbook of China) (Beijing: People's Republic of China Statistical Bureau, 1990), pp. 56, 363.

43. *Statistical Yearbook of China, 1991,* p. 65.

44. *Zhongguo Tongji Nianjian, 1984,* pp. 460, 464; *Zhongguo Tongji Nianjian, 1990,* p. 140.

45. Wang Hongmuo, *The Process of Reform and Openness* (in Chinese) (Hunan: Hunan Publishing House 1989), p. 14, quoted in Gong Ting, *Politics of Corruption,* p. 109.

46. *Zhongguo Tongji Nianjian, 1990,* p. 140.

47. Ethridge, *Unfinished Revolution,* p. 37; Cheng Chu-yuan, "China's Economic Reform at the Crossroads," in *Changes in China: Party, State, and Society,* ed. Shao-chuan Leng, p. 152 (New York: University Press of America, 1989).

48. *Statistical Yearbook of China, 1991,* p. 270.

49. Ethridge, *Unfinished Revolution,* pp. 46, 120.

50. *Statistical Yearbook of China, 1991,* p. 156.

51. Shao-chuan Leng, ed. *Changes in China,* p. 149 f.

52. *China's Statistical Abstract, 1989,* p. 91.

53. Ibid.

3

Socialist Mode of Corruption

Chinese socialist society has three distinguishing characteristics: monopoly of power held by the Communist Party, state ownership of property, and central planning of production.[1] As we have seen in chapter 2, between 1949 and 1989 China was marked mainly in the consolidation and gradual development of these features, punctuated by a slight loosening in the last decade. The Communist Party held real power in governance even though other "democratic" parties existed. Some properties were privately owned, but the means of production largely belonged to the state. For most of the period under review, central authorities set the production targets and guaranteed the supply of raw materials and distribution. Even in the more liberal atmosphere of the eighties, most production units played a minor role in regulating their production process.

In this chapter, I examine how these basic socialist features shaped the expression of corruption in China between 1949 and 1989. We shall examine not only how each of these characteristics left its separate marks on corruption, but also how they interacted with each other to provide opportunities for particular kinds of illegitimate activities making the phenomenon of corruption in China more like those in other socialist countries than in the capitalist West. Furthermore, because of our interest in how the distinctive character of socialism shapes corruption, we shall analyze the forty years of Chinese socialism as a static whole, ignoring the subtle differences over time.

Despite China's shared characteristics with other socialist societies, a country that has four thousand years of history has unique cultural traditions which shape social practices prompting some socialist scientists to analyze exclusively how these practices impinge on corruption. Mayfair Yang, for example, has explored how particularistic and patriarchal values shaped gift giving, a practice which can easily merge into the gray area of corruption.[2] Furthermore, China is also at its own stage of economic development distinct from other countries. The nature of the resources available affects the valuation of goods, and the opportunities structured by the level of her development can determine the ways corrupt officials benefit themselves. These cultural traditions and economic characteristics will make their imprints on the practices as they have on the meanings of corruption. In the following pages we shall examine how these diverse forces interact with the three socialist characteristics—the Communist Party, state ownership of property, and central planning—to make certain forms of corruption predominant in China.

The Power of the Communist Party

The Communist Party monopolized power at both the national and the grass-roots levels. It held political power in state governance; all the major decisions and the control of resources were party prerogatives. In addition, the infiltration of party power into every organization effectively controlled the individual. The presence of party and administrative control within each organization meant that workers were supervised by two authorities. Both chains of command were characterized by one-man governance, with a strict line of authority emanating from the top. Conflict between the two authorities was minimal because party power was greater than that of the administration. The latter bent to the will of the former. Sometimes even minor differences between these two sources of authority were avoided when the posts of administrative head and party secretary were held by the same person. Under these circumstances, *yiyuanhua lingdao* (unified leadership) was in its purest form. Even when the two posts were not held by one person, when these two lines of authorities worked in close cooperation, they acted like pincers to keep the individuals in place by enforcing the organizational rules and detecting and punishing any deviations on the part of the economic work units.

Vertical control over workers was further strengthened by the work unit's comprehensive authority over every aspect of the individual's life. Andrew Walder's study of neo-traditionalism in the industrial work unit and Jean Oi's analysis of the village exposed the impact of total control on the incumbents.[3] In the first few years of Communist rule, the production unit provided each worker's basic needs supplemented by a small stipend. Soon the salary system was introduced, but work units continued to supply eating facilities, housing, education, health, welfare, and other amenities at subsidized rates and often were the only conduit to obtain these supplies. Besides authorization from the work unit was required to travel, to buy a train ticket, to check into a hotel, to get married, to transfer to another work unit, to locate in another area, and, depending on the population policy of the time, to have a child. Individuals had few, sometimes no other, alternatives to satisfy their needs except what was available through the work unit. Obviously, because these authorizations, opportunities, and amenities were granted by one's immediate supervisor, there was a strong inducement for the staff to follow his/her directives.

The proclivity to corruption under socialism did not stem so much from the Communist Party's staying power, as it did from the fact that the ruling group held a monopoly of power. It could have been a party with any other name or political orientation. There is some truth in the adage that power corrupts and absolute power corrupts absolutely. In China the concentration of power in the unit heads at each level offered them more social assets, greater ability to extort from their subordinates, more opportunities to indulge in different kinds of corruption, and less chance of detection compared to their counterparts in more democratic forms of governance. In true democracies, power vested in administrative staff is generally more limited and circumscribed by a system of checks and balances so as to prevent blatant abuses;

moreover, administrative operations are policed by a separate and independent authority.

The way power was concentrated in China affected corruption in five distinct ways. First, the dependence on the higher authority for resources encouraged managers to inflate their needs to obtain more supplies. Second, the strong pressure to conform encouraged them and their subordinates to fabricate reports on their achievements to please those above. Third, the ability of supervisors to dispense resources offered opportunities for bribes—subordinates would give anything to get what they needed. Fourth, the control of resources also offered administrators opportunities to use them for their own benefit. And fifth, the people's dependence on these officials discouraged them from reporting illegal activities, thus increasing the anonymity of corrupt officials.

A bureaucracy dependent on a rigid hierarchy and without alternative resources tends to exaggerate its needs to protect its interests. Grass-root units in China did not behave any differently. The administrative staffs of production units tended to overreport their input requirements and underreport their capacity. These strategies lowered the performance expectations of the central government, gave administrators more room to maneuver in case of the unexpected, and made it easier for them to overfulfill their production targets.[4] Every level of every ministry tried to minimize its responsibilities and maximize its resources. This practice is not peculiar to socialism but to government bureaucracies dependent entirely on those above for support. Government departments in the West tend to inflate their budget estimates to forestall cuts from above as well. But in socialist countries, where every organization, including the production units, relies on the government, such practices are more prevalent and come to be associated with the socialist system. I shall discuss this problem in greater detail later in relation to central planning in production.

The organization's complete hold over the individual stemming from the socialist structure generated the pressure to conform, and this tendency was further strengthened by the emphasis on hierarchical order and the status orientation of China's traditional culture.

Those holding subordinate positions, whether by virtue of their age, wealth, or position, were expected to show unquestioning obedience and deference to their superiors. In this work situation, with the unequal power relationships and complete dependence on superiors, members of the organization were pressured by pragmatic considerations and encouraged by traditional culture to demonstrate formal, if not real, compliance with organizational expectations even though sometimes the means to attain these goals were beyond their reach. Thus, this often resulted in the problem of false reporting.

An example of the trouble the lower echelons would go to please their superiors was the visit of the provincial health inspector to the city of Qiqihar, Heilongjiang, in 1983. These local officials' motivations probably went beyond sheer compliance to include maintaining face or impression management, so important in the Chinese culture.[5] When the inspector came, Qiqihar looked surreal. The city government had put "a spitoon and a waste paper basket every 35 steps." When passersby would use the spitoons and waste paper baskets, they were told politely, "Sorry, you can't use it now." Booths were set up along the streets with speakers disseminating health information. Street cleaners even picked up leaves as soon as they fell from the trees. The day before the visit, a flower bed was put over the dirt outside the public latrines. On the day the inspector came, peasants were barred from the city and vendors confined to the side streets. Restaurant waiters were given swatters to fight flies, and fresh meat replaced the frozen variety usually available in the stores. All these improvements disappeared once the investigation team left.[6] Similar attempts at window dressing were made in the economic sector. In *The Private Life of Chairman Mao*, his doctor, Li Zhisui, recounted how communes transplanted and tightly packed wheat plants along the track that Mao's train would travel to demonstrate their compliance with the policies of the Great Leap Forward and their success.[7]

Ironically, the monopoly of power and its attendant efforts to extract conformity resulted in false reporting and cheating, because the negative consequences of nonconformity were high and the payoffs from meeting expectations were great. Although occasionally there were the humorous surrealistic improvisations for official visits, grass-roots units more often fabricated production statistics and submitted only positive reports to please their superiors. When the perceptive subordinates saw their superiors enthusiastic about new policies, such as the agricultural collectivization of the Great Leap Forward, they were especially willing and eager to comply.[8]

Administrators manipulated their production figures as the situation required. The actions of a Sichuan coal company in 1953 were typical. To qualify for the Red Flag prize for productivity, it reported coal output of 3,000 tons in October, which just met the required quota; they put aside another unreported 2,491 tons to cover future shortfalls.[9]

Others simply fabricated their production records or declared their low-quality goods of high quality to win praise from Beijing.[10] Between 1972 and 1979, the Guocai Furnace Company won several prizes for using less steel, less coke, and less electricity, when it was really using twice the national norm of steel and its heating capacity was 14 percent less than was reported.[11] In the rural areas, local cadres harvested grain from several fields they cleared in less accessible areas and combined the production, claiming it as harvest from a "model" plot with high yield.[12]

In centrally planned economies, target production quotas are built on information supplied from below. When the output figures are unreliable, the production targets built from this information are unattainable and impractical; attempts to implement these unrealistic central plans only strain the economy and production suffers. What occurred during the Great Leap Forward and the subsequent "three years of disaster" (1960–1962), when China was plagued by famine and starvation, were good examples of the disastrous consequences of false reporting. Aside from the inherent weaknesses of these policies, the inflated output figures supplied by many local cadres in the late fifties fed the vicious spiral—the center set ever higher production targets with each encouraging report. The continued optimism and false hopes prolonged the implementation of a hasty and unrealistic program that brought serious setbacks to the economy.

In this restrictive environment, some cadres inflated outputs even when their action clearly harmed work unit members. In agriculture, each production team gave the state a certain proportion of its harvest. When it inflated its output to qualify for the Red Flag prize or other such honors, the team had to provide higher grain procurement to the state as well. Some teams tried to compensate for the difference by opening new agricultural lands and not reporting the additional acreage to the higher-ups.[13] But if the actual production fell short of the reported one, the additional amount had to be taken from that set aside for the members; therefore, individual household consumption dropped. This was how one team remained an advanced unit between 1972 and 1975, when the grain distributed to each family dropped from 110 to 68 *jin*.[14]

In these examples, the cadres made good impressions on their superiors, but the reports did not suggest that they received any direct material benefits. But they could do so if they so chose. As long as state employees provide services or goods as part of their duties, they have the opportunity to use these items as capital for personal gains. No matter how limited their authority, administrative staff members are at a decided advantage vis-à-vis those working under them; the more power they have, the greater their clout. This chasm between the official prerogative and the powerlessness and dependence of the ruled opened up opportunities for bribery and extortion.[15]

The comprehensiveness of the power vested in state employees under socialism further increased those opportunities and made such officials likely targets for bribery. The more resources they controlled, and the fewer available from alternative sources, the more often people would appeal to them for help. Illegal payments were willingly given as long as the officials could deliver the wanted commodities, amenities, or services. Some showered officials with gifts to ensure that their requests would be granted when the time came; others would pay when the circumstances required. Whichever way it went, many felt it was worth their while because the returns often outweighed their investments. Often, a price could not be attached to these returns, but if it was available the amount paid was usually lower than that set at the official rate. For example, a state company that was to be fined nine million yuan for the late delivery of goods had the amount reduced to seven hundred thousand yuan, saving the company 8.3 million yuan, after giving the official in charge a bribe. The amount of the bribe was not reported but it was unlikely to be 8.3 million yuan.[16] Treating cadres investigating rural local units to banquets and giving them gifts could be costly too, but cultivating good relations with them could considerably reduce these units' annual grain procurement quotas to the state or convince them to turn a blind eye to blatant trangressions.[17] Moreover, the unit and not the individual footed the bill.

All else being equal, state employees with power and access to resources have many opportunities to divert them for their own comfort or benefit. In China, the special status of officials vis-à-vis the population rested not on their personal wealth but on the degree of power they enjoyed. Consequently they had more opportunities not only to receive bribes but also to misappropriate state resources in other ways. Sometimes dishonest officials threatened to delay or withhold services or goods unless their clients paid. People complied because they knew their loss might be greater if they did not pay. They would not get their entitlements or would be continually harassed in other ways.

The effect of the concentration of power was most obvious when one focuses on such abuses in the rural areas, where the central government's power was weaker and the authority of the local official more absolute and comprehensive than in the urban areas. In the early fifties, dishonest cadres buying grain for the state imposed a price lower than the official one on the peasants, or they cheated by using a measure that took in more than the specified amount; they pocketed the differences themselves. In 1956, Commune Number 38 in Da Xian lost 35 of their 3,781 *jin* of green hemp, while Commune Number 28 lost 241 yuan in this way.[18] Later, when peasants were paid in work points, cadres used a different method

to enrich themselves. Cadres below the commune level technically were not state employees and had to work on the land as
the other peasants. Instead, the state provided them grain coupons and subsidies when they left their farm duties to attend
meetings or take on other administrative responsibilities. Since
these cadres often were responsible for distributing the work
points, unethical ones "ate two portions," awarding themselves
both state stipends and work points for their nonexistent farm
labor. In one case, a cadre gave himself, in addition to his administrative stipends, two hundred days' work points, the equivalent of the number received by a family with two workers in a
year.[19] But the arrogance of these rural cadres was most obvious
in minor incidents in which they exercised their authority to
meet their personal and minor needs by inconveniencing everyone else. In one case, a cadre stopped all the trains in the locality
so his son could bring his bride back on the train at a "propi-
tious" time. On another occasion, an official in charge of the
power supply, worthy of the label of *dianba* (power hooligan),
could not get into a movie theater because the tickets were sold
out. In a rage, he returned to his office and simply shut off the
power to the theater.[20]

Such actions were certainly public knowledge, but few people
would bother to complain officially. Rural cadres controlled
every aspect of the peasants' life. They distributed collective
goods, allocated housing, assigned jobs, regulated their private
lives, and dispensed justice—they could make life miserable for
the peasants, if they so chose. If urban dwellers had difficulties
finding alternative channels for satisfying their needs or reporting
on the cadre, isolated rural inhabitants had a harder time. The
peasants like their urban counterparts knew what went on, but
they were too timid to question official misdemeanor. Traditionally, local officials were the *fumu guan,* literally translated as
parental official. At its best, the term reflected the officials' concern for their charges, but even at its best it signified the paternal-
ism that characterized governance. The local officials were the
"parents," and as parents their authority was beyond question;

peasants were only to obey. But in the decades prior to Communist rule, dishonest officials often behaved like local mafias, milking and bullying their wards to satisfy their avarice. If the peasants wanted to complain, they had no higher authority to turn to. They suffered in silence. The Communist government restored law and order, but now the local cadre was the investigator, judge, and dispenser of justice rolled into one. Workers and peasants rarely broke out from their habituation to silence and, if they did, they had nowhere to turn to locally unless they went over the cadres to report to their superiors outside the village or their work units. Even then, their chances of success were not assured. The folk sayings *Guan ze liang ge kou* (the written character for "official" indicates two mouths, i.e., officials are more articulate and are better able to convince) and *Guan guan sheng wei* (officials are solicitous of each other's well-being) describe the suspicion and insecurity traditionally felt by those confronting government officials. Consequently, the average Chinese only complained to each other.[21]

According to game theory, often used to explain political and economic action, actors are more likely to engage in an action if the gains of participation outweigh nonparticipation, when the probability of success exceeds that of failure, and when the chances of getting away with it are greater than those of getting caught. These same factors can explain Chinese corruption in general, as well as the audacity of many cadres in exploiting their positions. Corrupt action certainly brings more personal gains; with the concentration of power in the hands of the officials, the chances of getting caught are not high and those of success are great.

This situation is not unique to Communist rule. Chinese officials have traditionally enjoyed inordinate powers and their subordinates have practiced the code of silence. Through the system of unified leadership, Communist leaders reinforced such practices, and the monopoly of power in the government bureaucracy became more entrenched. The resulting vertical and horizontal monopoly of power, sanctioned by traditional as well as the Marxist ideology, exerted pressure on the cadres to conform through fair means or foul; it offered them the opportunities to commit misdemeanors, but also encouraged apathy and coverup from their subordinates, thus providing state employees with a certain degree of immunity from detection or exposure.

State Ownership of Property

The prohibition against private ownership sets most socialist societies apart from capitalist ones. The Chinese state owned the major means of production. Factories were state-owned and farmlands were collective property. Individuals might own the clothes on their backs, the furniture in their houses, or other household items and small possessions, but they did not own, until the 1980s, any major consumer items (such as houses or motor cars) or any means of production that could bring in large profit.

Ownership is the most basic form of a person's relationship to property; from it devolves the rights of usage, profit, and transfer. In socialist countries, all property belongs to the state. Aside from owning the property, the state also organizes the means of production, draws profit from the country's resources, and redistributes the returns to its subunits. Despite the practice of central planning, the central government has to delegate the rights of usage and transfer to civil servants to carry out their responsibilities. These prerogatives of state employees become their social assets or intangible property rights in a society that delegitimizes private ownership.[22] These state employees enjoy informal property rights, such as the rights to use and dispense state resources, by virtue of their official position subject, however, to regulation by the state.

These characteristics of socialism regarding property rights interacted with the peculiarities of the Chinese social context to give the Chinese form of corruption two distinct and contradictory features. First, the absence of private property, together with scarce economic resources, largely discouraged bribery and extortion cases involving large monetary values. Second, the delegation of authority over property rights, together with the concentration of power in the administrative staff, encouraged the acceptance of bribes, wastage, and other abuses of public property.

With the low level of economic development and the banning of private property in the period of classical socialism, Chinese citizens had little to offer officials when they chose to try to bribe them. The gifts offered were generally of little economic value: wine, food, pots, pans, utensils, clothing materials, blankets, and local produce that was difficult to obtain from the stores but would add to the officials' daily comforts.[23] But even when the clients offered valuable articles, state employees were reluctant to accept them. With the absence of private property and the condemnation of any ostentatious display of private wealth, many material possessions such as gold, jewelry, and other luxury items lost much of their attraction. On the contrary, having such possessions could draw unwanted attention to any illegal transactions.

With the liberalization of economic policies, and the corresponding tolerance of private ownership and acceptance of material comforts that accompanied the growing prosperity of the eighties, the value of the items used for graft increased tremendously, especially in sectors where huge profits could be made. The role of money in these illicit activities assumed greater importance. In the absence of the market in the first three decades of Communist rule, money lost much of its liquidity because, with few goods available in the stores, it could not be exchanged for what one wanted and was therefore of little use as a bribe. In addition, the devaluation of money discouraged embezzlement of public funds, so that such occurrences were rare and the amounts stolen averaged only a few hundred yuan.[24] But in the eighties, cash bribes and embezzlement became common and the amounts escalated to the hundreds of thousands.

Unlike the bourgeoisie or capitalists who own their factories or farms, socialist state employees are custodians of resources, not owners. The former group would care for their property because, more often than not, this serves as their means to generate personal income. In the latter situation, just as everybody's responsibility is no one's responsibility, state property belonging to everyone in the abstract is nobody's property. State officials only manage the property. They do not share the property owners' commitment to the resources under their charge. In the paternalistic Chinese socialist society, where the central government takes good care of production units, soft budget constraint is practiced; Chinese officials know that the central government will bail out any losing businesses. Unlike the bourgeoisie, these Chinese administrators do not depend for their livelihood on the performance of the factory or farm that they manage, but rather on how they relate with their superiors.

This attitude leads to the problem of waste, which plagues most socialist countries. Oi recounted how an average of twenty *jin* of grain per *mu* were left in the fields at harvest, when crops were being weighed and reported to the state; however, once the official harvesting was over, peasants gleaned the field to recover the grain.[25] The story of the warehouse guard who left refrigerators worth seven million yuan in the open air to clear a room for his own sewing machine is another clear example of the priority given to private versus public property in a socialist society, and the havoc this mentality among the custodians of state property can bring to an already weak economy.[26]

The lack of commitment to safeguard state property made state officials easy targets for bribery. Again, game theory applies here. In the abstract, state property might be everyone's property, but few felt that way. In dispensing favors for a fee, state officials gave away something that did not belong to them in exchange for something personal and tangible and would belong to them. They would lose only if they were found out, and it was unlikely that their clients would tell. The earlier story about the official whittling down a fine from nine million to seven hundred thousand yuan was a good example of how officials gave away state property. The state lost 8.3 million yuan, much more than what this person gained. The same mentality also explained the contracts signed in the eighties between state enterprises and foreign business companies, in which officials representing state firms willingly agreed to pay high prices for inferior goods, or other such settlements favoring the foreign private business after receiving some *houzhu* or good things, from the other party.[27]

As mentioned earlier, stealing public or private property in a socialist state did not necessarily guarantee the opportunity to enjoy them. Consequently, many unethical Chinese administrative officials did not pocket the resources under their charge, but instead enjoyed them on the job, ignoring administrative regulations. They abused the power of usage delegated to them. The result was almost as good as owning the resources; however, unlike the owners, they did not have to worry about maintaining or renewing these resources.

Chinese popular culture seemed tolerant of such practices, as evidenced in the popular sayings: "Those who live near the water and the terrace see the moon first"; "Those who cross the river will get their feet wet"; or "If a person sells meat and doesn't eat it, he might as well be a carpenter." In other words, one might as well seize the opportunity when it presents itself. Traditional culture condemned corruption, but traditional culture was neither homogeneous nor inherently consistent. This opportunistic value in popular culture undermined the state's demand for integrity and honesty from officials.

There were the Chinese traditions of holding banquets on official occasions and providing the appropriate rites of welcome for visiting officials. Lower officials who did not live up to these expectations would lose face. These traditions remained strong under Communist rule. Only now, Chinese officials used these traditions to their advantage by throwing huge banquets at public expense to curry the favor of their superiors and for their own enjoyment. They used discretionary funds to cover these expenses or fabricated receipts to hide the illicit transfers. Some state employees splurged with public money on justifiable business trips, or went on questionable ones and used the opportunity to sightsee or to buy consumer goods not available in their hometowns.[28] In 1953, the manager of a food company spent three million yuan on his official travel, some of the money was used to pay for long distance telephone calls to his wife. Moreover, he took two million yuan worth

of goods from the warehouses he visited.[29] Under reform socialism, there were many reports of officials who took the entire
family along on trips; some even brought private nurses, cooks,
and photographers.[30]

Managerial staff managers in positions of authority put public
money into capital expenditures to better their own working and
living conditions. Between 1953 and 1954, the manager of
Xinhua Factory spent 22,400 yuan on twenty-three unauthorized
items for his own use, including a house, bicycles, motor cars,
and a chauffeur.[31] Another factory manager built living quarters
consisting of only eighty-eight units of over eighty-one square
meters each for his senior staff, when the factory had seven hundred workers, majority of whom were married and waiting for
accommodations.[32] The practice continued into the eighties with
administrators building more luxurious clubhouses and apartments
for themselves and their families. The repeated warnings in the
state-run media against the abuse of and wastefulness in public
funds only confirmed the rampancy of such practices and the
government's failure to halt the misuse of discretionary funds.

Central Planning of Production

In theory, central planning in production, which allows the top
leadership to establish a monopoly of economic power, enables it
to optimize the use of national resources, and coordinate and
balance diverse regional interests. The local units state their needs
and production capacities; the center sets the production targets,
supplies the resources, and guarantees the market. In practice,
central planning involves a process of intense negotiation between the upper and lower levels. The upper levels pressure the
lower units to provide high outputs with low inputs, and the
lower levels as described in the earlier section attempt to squeeze
as many resources from above as possible, while setting the lowest performance targets, until a final compromise is reached.[33]

With their dependence on the center and in the absence of a
market economy, industries in socialist countries lack the elastic-

ity or flexibility enjoyed by businesses in capitalist societies, with their multiple sources of supply and many outlets. If these socialist organizations overestimate their needs and underestimate their productive capacity, they can increase their reserves and provide room to manipulate in case of the unexpected, put less pressure on their workers, and enhance their chances of meeting the targets.

These preservation instincts under central planning are further enhanced by the shortages of supplies often experienced by socialist societies. Inadequate planning based on unreliable information has often resulted in inefficiency in production, scarcity of goods, inappropriateness of the supplies, bottlenecks, late deliveries, delivery of the wrong supplies, and nondelivery. The resulting shortages are all the more aggravating because many countries with low production capability had only turned to socialism out of economic desperation. China is no exception. In 1949, the country was ravaged by decades of foreign invasion and internal strife. It was a Third World country with scarce resources and low production capacity, suffering from a shortage economy accentuated by socialist structures. Production units were plagued by inadequate supplies, late deliveries, or delivery of materials that did not meet specifications, all of which could result in work stoppages.[34] For the production units, overreporting seemed to be the cheapest and most efficient solution to these problems.

Units that over-estimated their budgets, underreported their inventories, ordered more than required, underassessed their production capacity, and did not report all their output, would have money and raw materials left over at the end of the fiscal year.[35] Like their counterparts in other socialist countries, Chinese administrators adopted these strategies to make life easier for themselves. Also like these counterparts, they were most reluctant to return any surplus. Some would simply falsified their records. In the early fifties when the free market still existed, bureaucrats colluded with merchants in predating or forging receipts. More cautious ones would spend their money even on things that might be useless or redundant before the center could reclaim it. In 1956, a sugar factory with ninety workers bought eighty double beds, 150 single beds, and 120 desks, giving each worker two and a half beds and 1.3 desks.[36]

The unreported surplus stock went into storage for later use. Steel was always a scarce commodity and hoarding it was most widespread. For example, at the end of the 1959 fiscal year, Gansu Province had enough steel planks, good quality steel, shaped steel, steel wires, and other steel products to meet its needs for half a year. In 1971, Wusi Compressor Factory had 3,800 tons of steel that could last it for a year and a half.[37] The vice party secretary of Henan was accused of underreporting production of 5.3 million tons of coal between 1974 and 1976, hiding 1.7 million tons of cement and 16,000 machines from the center between 1972 and 1976, and not reporting 32,900 tractors and 770 cars between 1973 and 1976.[38] The frequent calls by the media for units to "clear their stocks" attested to the prevalence of hoarding and the futility of government efforts to stamp it out.

Besides steel and other capital goods, units stockpiled anything and everything in this land of scarcity. They might use the goods in their warehouses for production or exchange them for other needed items. Bartering was a common practice in less developed economies. In China, production units bypassed the official distribution channels and bartered to facilitate production needs. Some even had standing agreements with each other to avoid the trouble of searching for supply units each time they needed something. As early as 1958, a factory in Zhangjiakou in Hebei had a tacit arrangement with several other units to exchange soldering tubes and various grades of steel for steel threads, wood, compressors, cement, and galvanized iron plate.[39]

Because supplies were inelastic, production units manufacturing goods in demand could behave in the same way as dishonest state officials who demanded extra payments and other special treatments for things they could offer. Some units required their clients to supply them with raw materials when they put in their orders. Even after their clients fulfilled their obligations, these units often delayed production or delivery, and exchanged the raw materials so obtained for other goods they needed. Consumers of the eighties suffered under this system too. Sometimes they could get what they wanted only if they would also purchase less popular items. A person needing a pack of cigarettes might have to buy meat, fish, garlic, oil, or some other food as well; another person needing a spitoon might have to take ten pairs of chopsticks. A customer buying a 1,700–yuan Double Deer brand refrigerator had to pay 2,500 yuan because he also had to buy the Meteor brand receiver.[40] Imposing such conditions came close to extortion, but with scarce supplies, managers of the few sources of supplies could force these conditions on their clients to benefit their units and get away with it.

Most studies on corruption in socialist countries have focused mainly on bribery and extortion, ignoring the many other forms of corruption identified in this chapter. Yang saw gift giving and bribery as forms of resistance in which circulation of goods in the free space beyond the reach of state control was created.[41] David Bayley and Nathaniel Leff viewed these two forms of corruption as a means to ease bottlenecks and facilitate the circulation of goods, because they allowed those who could afford and needed the goods to have access to them.[42] To that, we can add that extortion allows manufacturers to get rid of their surplus stocks, forcing unwanted goods on their clients.

Coming from the opposite perspective, the Chinese government condemned these practices not as expressions of freedom but as insubordination. They saw these actions not as a means to facilitate, but a means to obstruct the circulation of goods. To them, bribery and extortion were not only wrong but also undermined central planning, by diverting materials away from those units/individuals that rightfully should have them to those better endowed, and hurt national economic interests. Furthermore, hoarding materials whether for the purpose of attracting or giving bribes increased the turnover time of materials and capital from the estimated two months to an average of six months. According to official estimates, the number of hoarded or "stagnated" capital items could rise to as high as 42 percent of the total in circulation. It was a vicious circle. When scarce goods were withdrawn from circulation and stockpiled in warehouses, shortages became worse, and sometimes waste ensued. Iron rusted, cotton rotted, and perishables went bad. When goods remained in storage and left to waste, other factories lacking these supplies were forced to stop production.[43] For all these reasons, the Chinese government condemned bureaucratism, corruption, and waste all in the same directive.

Organizational Corruption

Corrupt officials generally gained personally from their transgressions. But in many of the examples of corruption mentioned in the last section, such as hoarding, bribery, and extortion, the organization and not the individual stood to benefit—state employees broke regulations in the interests of their organizations. The pressure for managerial staff to commit such organizational crime is stronger in China than in the capitalist countries, where sometimes corporate executives break the law to benefit their companies. This pressure arises in part from the socialist structures and, ironically, is also encouraged by socialist ideology.

As described earlier, the individual's reliance on the organization for his/her every need, together with the limited mobility brought on by the practice of life-time employment, has induced a strong and enduring sense of commitment to the work unit. After all, if the units prospered so would the members. Similarly, the organizational arrangements and the resulting commitment to the organizations' well-being, as we have seen, encouraged managers in the lower echelons to use the power delegated to them to indulge in certain forms of organizational corruption, such as misrepresenting their needs and performance and hiding their surplus from their superiors. They also dealt with horizontal organizations in extralegal ways, such as bartering, to satisfy their wants and to increase their revenue.[44]

Such organizational corruption, as filing false reports and other forms of cheating the upper echelons, is possible only if the socialist system does not have a good monitoring system. Ironically, this is the case. Despite the reputation of a socialist society being tightly controlled, individual organizations have relative autonomy if they operate or pretend to operate within the official guidelines and satisfy their superiors with appropriate reports. Organization members are under the close scrutiny of their supervisors, and organizations have cumbersome bookkeeping procedures, but there are few, if any, agencies or effective procedures to control inventory or to monitor or audit the overall functioning of these organizations. The leaders of organizations are left very much on their own. Investigation teams visit these units occasionally, but the units usually are given notice, which allows them time to prepare for such visits. On the one hand, the upper echelons put pressure on the lower units to comply with their targets and guidelines; on the other, they have few methods to authenticate the factuality of such reports, or enough time to investigate the situation locally. Often the investigation teams are preoccupied with the protocols of hospitality which leave little time for on-site investigation.

The solidarity of these organizations created under socialism and the traditional strong sense of localism vis-à-vis the outsiders do not make the work of these investigators easy. In developing countries where cooperation among neighbors is essential for survival, communities are close-knit and the sense of identity strong. In China, this community spirit remains vibrant. Members are loyal to their work units as well as to their localities, and are unlikely to tell strangers anything especially when illicit activities are involved. After all, there is the adage, "Anything that brings shame to the family should not be repeated outside." Anyone who breaks this norm is bringing shame to the unit or locality too. He/she will be ostracized and will pay when the investigation team leaves.

The philosophy of a socialist society rests on the pursuit of the collective good; therefore, the interest of the larger unit is always a concern for administrative personnel. The Communist Party's monopoly of power, the abolition of private property, and central planning are premised precisely on this belief. Private property has to be suppressed because it is an expression of individual interest and an aberration of the collective one. The assumption of a monopoly of power by one party committed to socialism is the means for balancing individual interests and for achieving collective well-being. Central planning in production is the means for attaining utopia in the economic sector.

In practice, a person's sense of collectivity is shaped by one's social location. The social locations of the different levels of the managerial staff provide them varying interpretations of the collective and distinct unit priorities. To central leaders, collective interest is the national interest. To provincial officials, the province is often their unit of concern. At the county level, county interest is paramount. The slogan "working for the people," in reality, is translated into safeguarding the interests of the members of a particular work unit. This "misguided" sense of collectivity is what the Chinese central government condemned as "mountaintopism" (*shantouzhuyi*), departmentalism (*benweizhuyi*), parochialism (*difangzhuyi*), "independent kingdoms" (*duli wangguo*), or the pursuit by managers of the unit's interests to the detriment of the collective interest. People who engaged in organizational corruption based on false reporting, bribery, extortion, the spending of public money on unnecessary and lavish capital investment, bartering, exhausting surplus allocations, and hoarding could console themselves that they were doing it for their organizations and not for themselves.

Using illicit methods to produce gains for their own units, with little concern for the larger picture, was prevalent in rural and urban areas and at every level of governance. For example, in the early fifties, the state bought grain from the rural areas, and cadres, to protect local interests, tried as much as possible to prevent grain from leaving their localities by exaggerating the amount of grain sold to the state. When there were good harvests and excess supplies, cadres divided up the grain among the peasants instead of selling it to the government. But they were most enthusiastic in selling state-owned produce to their communities, as in the case of a cadre from the sixth district of Dayixian. In 1954, he bought 1,700 *jin* from ten families supposedly for the state, but sold 166,310 *jin* to 239 of the 257 households under his jurisdiction instead.[45] And when some communes cleared new agricultural lands, they did not inform the state but kept the harvest for themselves.

In the urban areas, some officials inflated the number of employees to get more grain coupons or salary from the state. One official was caught reporting 780 instead of 648 workers eating in the plant cafeteria. The excess grain coupons were exchanged with the farmers by the cafeteria staff for wheat, beans, or other products with which to feed the workers.[46] Other work units provided conveniences for their staffs despite State Council directives warning against such practices. Department stores allowed their staffs to have first pick at newly arrived goods, and factories provided their workers products at cost. A factory in Shenyang was criticized for selling six hundred pairs of shoes to its workers at four to five yuan a pair, seven yuan below the production cost in 1976. The next year, the employees got another pair at 40 percent below the retail price.[47] In the eighties, factories withheld their profits from the state to replenish their "little till," or *xiaojinku*. The government limited the proportion of profit to be distributed to the workers as bonuses, but the regulations were often ignored or bypassed. When the state put caps on bonuses, managers gave workers overtime pay, hardship supplements, food supplements, water and electricity supplements, prizes for diligence, prizes for achievements, etc.[48] Fuzhou Department Store gave out 184,000 yuan as overtime pay and supplements to its workers organizing a meeting in 1984—they received an extra 6 yuan per diem, an additional 3 yuan for taking the evening shift, 3 yuan each time they received guests, 3 yuan for missing a meal, 9 yuan as a meal subsidy, and 3 yuan as lodging subsidy.[49]

Organizational corruption in socialist countries may be politically motivated. Ruan Ming, for example, believed that the leaders of Hainan Island smuggled cars, televisions, and other luxury items into the country only to benefit their region. Without the capital coming from the returns of these illicit operations, the region would not have developed so fast.[50] The accused may legitimize their activities in this way, but it will be difficult to establish whether the requirement for capital investment prompted these illicit actions or whether the outcomes were simply the unintended fallouts from the wealth amassed from these sources. Whichever the case, the local regions did benefit.

These illicit activities produced a steady supply of raw materials, smoother production, higher output, more housing units, nicer offices, better amenities, newer buildings, more conveniences and bonuses. Both the administrators and the workers benefited. As a result, no one had any reason except moral compunction to report such transgressions. Workers and administrators were simply bound together by mutual benefits within their collective unit into a culture of silence.

Pervasive Gray Corruption

Officials engaged in false reporting, bribery, misuse of public funds, defrauding the government, and other misdemeanors for their own interests and that of their organizations. Many more of these examples fall into the administrative definition of corruption than into the legal one, and can be categorized as gray rather than black corruption. The distinctive social organization of the Chinese socialist economy (with its monopoly of power by the Communist Party, the centralization of authority, the lack of divisions of functions within the organization, and, ironically, the absence of a means to enforce accountability) had prompted and allowed its officials to abuse their enormous administrative power, to break rules to accommodate the demands of higher echelons, to adopt questionable strategies to survive the inelastic and shortage socialist economy, and to protect the interests of their units.[51] Readers can easily point to similar occurrences of corruption in the West in which individuals broke comparable state laws or organizational rules to benefit themselves or their units. What sets China, and indeed other socialist countries, apart from the capitalist West is not any basic differences in the nature of corrupt activities but the salience and peculiar forms some of these activities have taken due to unique socialist structural arrangements.

A brief comparison of corruption in China and the capitalist West will highlight this point. First, Chinese socialist state officials fabricated reports to please their superiors. In the West's more democratic society, administrators feel much less compunction about catering to the demands and interests of their superiors. Because of the different ownership structure, many such reports would be of no interest to Western governments. If submitted, the authors would be reprimanded for fabrication and not accused of corruption. Second, socialist officials hoarded and bartered goods to avoid the consequences of inelasticity and scarcity of supplies, but administrators in Western economic units, with access to alternative if not better sources of supplies, generally do not have to use these methods to guarantee production. Third, in socialist China, where private property was banned and the level of development low, the acquisition of material items played a more important role than did monetary gain; however, in the more affluent and capitalist West, many administrators would not risk their positions for the small returns some Chinese officials received. Moreover, in the West money, and not material goods, is usually the ultimate goal of illicit transactions. Also, because private property was banned, Chinese officials were more likely to milk the state than the citizens simply because the former had more capital. To corrupt administrators in the West, everyone is a fair target. Fourth, given the strong dependence of the individual on the unit for his/her every need and the emphasis in socialist ideology on collective interest, together with the lack of outside monitoring agencies, crimes or misdemeanors to enhance the interest of the organization were more prevalent in socialist China than in the capitalist West, where organizational loyalty is much weaker. These differences in the social structure and level of development explain why we find false reporting, hoarding, and bartering common in China; they also explain the salience of organizational corruption and the predominance of material goods in these transactions.

Finally, the absence of certain forms of corruption in China tells us much about the effects on corruption of state control of the economy and the centralization of power. In the West, companies engaged in price fixing and inside trading are prosecuted, but in socialist China, where prices are set by the center and implemented by state companies, such concepts are alien and unknown. In China, prices are "regulated" and not "fixed" by the state to make these goods accessible to consumers; they are not tagged at high rates to obtain profit and in some cases these prices do not even cover production cost. Even in the nineties, no private conglomerates are strong enough to fix prices. Influence peddling and the bribing of lawmakers occur in the West where interest groups contribute money legitimately and illegitimately to powerbrokers. In China with its centralized control, clients bribe the executors of state policy; almost never the Beijing policy makers. The latter may be open to influences of their family members or close confidantes, but remain inaccessible to the ordinary citizens.

In short, while corruption in both socialist and capitalist societies is committed by those who wield power, their prizes, prey, and strategies are different conditioned by the economic structures of their societies. In China, socialist philosophies not only shape the meaning of corruption; but its structures define what goods are attractive, what actions are necessary, and what channels are feasible. Understanding such arrangements inside as well as outside the work organization is essential to an analysis of corruption in China.

Notes

1. Janos Kornai, *The Socialist System: The Political Economy of Communism* (Princeton: Princeton University Press, 1992), chapters 1 and 2.

2. Mayfair Mei-hui Yang, "The Gift Economy and State Power in China," *Comparative Studies in Society and History* 31, no. 1 (January 1989):25–54.

3. Andrew G. Walder, *Communist Neo-Traditionalism: Work and Authority in Chinese Industry* (Berkeley: University of California Press, 1986); Jean C. Oi, *State and Peasant in Contemporary China: The Political Economy of Village Government* (Berkeley: University of California Press, 1989).

4. *Sichuan Ribao,* February 20, 1956, p. 3.

5. Kwang-kuo Hwang. "Face and Favor: The Chinese Power Game," *American Journal of Sociology* 92:4 (January 1987): 944–74.

6. *Renmin Ribao,* September 8, 1983, p. 3.

7. Li Zhisui, *The Private Life of Chairman Mao* (New York: Random House, 1994).

8. *Sichuan Ribao,* February 20, 1956, p. 3.

9. *Sichuan Ribao,* March 31, 1953, p. 3.

10. *Renmin Ribao,* December 5, 1978, p.,1; February 24 1979, p. 2.

11. *Renmin Ribao,* September 20, 1980, p. 1.

12. Huang Shu-min, *The Spiral Road: Change in a Chinese Village Through the Eyes of a Communist Party Leader* (Boulder: Westview Press, 1989), pp. 60–61.

13. Ibid.

14. *Renmin Ribao,* July 7, 1979, p. 1.

15. James C. Scott, *Comparative Political Corruption* (Englewood Cliffs, N.J.: Prentice Hall, 1972), pp. 67–68.

16. Chen Nai-chao, *Zhonggong Tanwu Jiantao* (An examination of corruption in Communist China) (Hong Kong: Xin Shiji Chubanshe, 1953), p.83.

17. Oi, *State and Peasant,* p. 129.

18. *Sichuan Ribao,* June 20, 1953, p. 3; September 14, 1954, p. 3; August 13, 1956, p. 2.

19. *Sichuan Ribao,* October 27, 1962, p. 2, December 8, 1964, p. 1; *Renmin Ribao,* June 1, 1978, p. 1.

20. *Renmin Ribao,* October 19, 1981, p. 3; December 4, 1982, p. 5; July 3, 1983, p. 2; August 3, 1983, p. 8; August 11, 1983, p. 2; September 9, 1983, p. 2; Januay 7, 1984, p. 4; December 3, 1986, p. 1; June 18, 1987, p. 4; August 8, 1987, p. 1; August 16, 1987, p. 2; October 8, 1987, p. 2; November 21, 1987, p. 5; December 16, 1987, p. 4; January 17, 1988, p. 2; November 7, 1988, p. 1; December 3, 1988, p. 4; December 11, 1988, p. 2; December 16, 1988, p. 2; December 16, 1988, p. 4; December 23, 1988, p. 4.

21. See Huang Shu-min, *Spiral Road,* pp. 107–28.

22. N. Vijjay Jogannathan, *Informal Markets in Developing Countries* (New York: Oxford University Press, 1987), chapter 2.

23. *Renmin Ribao,* November 5, 1983, p. 5.

24. *Anhui Ribao,* July 24, 1956, p. 3; *Shaanxi Ribao,* January 12, 1958, p. 3; *Sichuan Ribao,* August 22, 1957, p. 2; August 7, 1958, p. 3.

25. Oi, *State and Peasant,* p. 119.

26. *Sichuan Ribao,* March 1, 1953, p. 3.

27. *Renmin Ribao,* July 27, 1982, p. 1; April 8, 1984, p. 1, cited in Peter Nan-shong Lee, "Bureaucratic Corruption During the Deng Xiaoping Era," *Corruption and Reform* 5 (1990):34.

28. *Sichuan Ribao,* July 12, 1955, p. 2.

29. *Sichuan Ribao,* February 21, 1953, p. 1; February 24, 1953, p. 2.

30. *Renmin Ribao,* September 19, 1979, p. 1; October 18, 1981, p. 5; January 8, 1984, p. 1; November 10, 1984, p. 5; March 14, 1987, p. 5; October 16, 1988, p. 8.

31. *Sichuan Ribao,* July 12, 1955, p. 2.

32. *Sichuan Ribao,* August 5, 1955, p. 2.

33. For details of this negotiation process, see Oi, *State and Peasant,* chapter 3.

34. *Sichuan Ribao,* August 13, 1955, p.1, reported that seventy-seven requests worth 26 million yuan submitted to the government in the first quarter of the year was overestimated by 1.64 million yuan.

35. *Sichuan Ribao,* December 27, 1956, p. 1; December 31, 1956, p. 1; December 18, 1962, p. 2; August 11, 1972, p. 3.

36. *Sichuan Ribao,* December 27, 1956, p. 1; December 31, 1956, p. 1; December 18, 1962, p. 2; December 19, 1971, p. 3.

37. *Renmin Ribao,* March 16, 1959, p. 3; July 20, 1978, p. 2.

38. *Renmin Ribao,* November 13, 1978, p. 1.

39. *Hebei Ribao,* November 6, 1958, p. 1.

40. *Renmin Ribao,* June 8, 1980, p. 3; June 12, 1980, p. 2; August 3, 1980, p. 3; August 31, 1983, p. 5; February 25, 1984, p. 2; September 20, 1986, p. 5.

41. Mayfair Mei-hui Yang, "Gift Economy," pp. 25–54.

42. Nathaniel Leff, "Economic Development Through Bureaucratic Corruption," *American Behavioral Scientist* 8, no. 3 (November 1964): 8–14; David Bayley, "The Effect of Corruption in Developing Nations," *Western Political Quarterly* 19, no. 4 (December 1966): 719–32, reprinted in Arnold J. Heidenheimer, Michael Johnston, and Victor T. Levine, *Political Corruption* (New Brunswick, N.J.: Transaction Books, 1990), pp. 935–52.

43. *Sichuan Ribao,* August 31, 1955, p. 2; *Renmin Ribao,* June 8, 1962, p. 1.

44. See Richard Madsen, *Morality and Power in a Chinese Village* (Berkeley: University of California Press, 1984), pp. 159–60, 173–74, on the different perceptions of collective interest in a Chinese village.

45. *Sichuan Ribao,* September 22, 1954, p. 3; October 16, 1954, p. 3.

46. *Sichuan Ribao,* August 19, 1955, p. 2; August 27, 1955, p. 2; December 7, 1957, p. 2; *Xinhua Monthly,* no. 12 (1955):230.

47. *Renmin Ribao,* April 8, 1978, p. 4; July 27, 1978, p. 4; November 7, 1978, p. 2.

48. *Renmin Ribao,* October 9, 1978, p. 2; November 6, 1980, p. 4; August 9, 1981, p. 1; February 5, 1984, p. 4; May 9, 1988, p. 2.

49. *Renmin Ribao,* August 18, 1987, p. 1.

50. Ruan Ming, *Deng Xiaoping: Chronicle of an Empire* (Boulder: Westview Press, 1994), p. 155.

51. Alan P.L. Liu, "The Politics of Corruption in the People's Republic of China," *American Political Science Review* 77, no. 3 (September 1983): 602–23.

4

Parabola of Corruption

In chapter 3, my analysis dealt with corruption in China between 1949 and 1989 as a static entity in order to understand how its various forms were shaped by Chinese socialist organizational structures. In this chapter, I examine the evolution of corruption in the same period focusing on the incidence, the goods being exchanged, their monetary values, the dominant forms of corruption, and the networks that were used.

This analysis suggests that China had a more honest government in the period of classical socialism than under reform socialism, when we witness the growth of corruption involving a higher incidence, greater sums of money, more varied forms, and a widening scope of involvement. However, if the forty years were taken as a continuous whole, development of corruption resembles a U-curve—corruption was serious when the Communist government took power, the problem was soon brought under control and rose again in the eighties to become a more serious problem than in the early fifties.

Guomindang Legacy of Corruption

Corruption was one of the many reasons for the fall of the Guomindang in 1949. Toward the end of the Republican period (1911–1949), corruption occurred on a wide scale and involved a large number of the officials at every rank and in almost every arena of government work. Public offices were openly bought and sold, and the going rates were public information. For example, three thousand yuan would buy the office of a district magistrate in Jiangxi for three months between 1930–1933.[1] Since holding office was a business investment, the incumbents tried to recover the cost and make a profit during their tenure. Since looking after the interest of kin and family was deemed important in Chinese society, these government officials, like proprietors in Chinese firms, positioned their relatives or friends in lucrative government offices as well so they too could benefit. These officials ran the government as if they were operating businesses, only they probably had more power than the business people.

Historically, Chinese officials have had great power over the people. In the best of circumstances, they were the "parent-officials" (*fumu guan*) who made every decision and looked after the population's every need. On the other hand, bad officials could easily misuse their prerogatives and exploit the obeisance and compliance of their wards. In the late Republican period, it was common for officials to confiscate private property, as it was to demand for payment from their clients before discharging their official duties. Businesses usually had to pay the relevant state employees to avoid harassment or to get prompt or needed services.[2] Some tax collectors invented levies and surcharges well above the official rate.[3] When grain was the form of payment, some officials underestimated the quality and weight of the crops the peasants provided. Others took into consideration the volatile political situation and collected taxes well ahead of time. In one case, taxes were assessed forty years ahead and collected ten to twenty years in advance.[4] When a worker was drafted to work on an official's private project, he had to pay to get out of such an illegally imposed corvee. Oftentimes, the victims were not cognizant of their rights. Even if they were, they were usually too powerless to resist the officials' demands.

The politically powerful embezzled public funds, and foreign aid for public projects went into their private pockets. Dishonest grain collectors at every level skimmed off the top of their collections; some added sand and pebbles to make up for the difference in weight, and others claimed that the entire stock was lost to spillage, robbery, or accidents while it was being transported. When citizens were conscripted for public projects, corrupt government officials inflated their numbers to qualify for additional allocations. However, unlike some socialist officials studied in chapter 3 who reported more workers to provide better food rations for their existing staff or re-invested the illicit gains into the region, these Republican officials pocketed the difference and sometimes even the larger share of the allowances, leaving the conscripts hungry and weak.[5]

Besides these blatant forms of corruption, unethical officials also enriched themselves through legal but morally questionable means. Some collaborated with merchants in speculation by providing the merchants with information on projected scarcity of certain goods; the merchants would then buy up the goods, further driving up artificially the prices for the consumers. Other officials would lend the merchants transportation facilities under their charge to bring goods from places where the prices were low to sell in areas where they commanded higher prices. Still other officials went into business for themselves. Because they controlled public resources, and sometimes also the means of transportation, they were able to turn these assets into capital for trading or speculation.

Toward the end of the Republican period, many public officials became primarily servants of the rich. Adequate cash payments could silence local officials, persuade them into action or inaction, and even effectively cover up any criminal offenses or secure the release of prisoners. This rampant corruption undermined the effectiveness and legitimacy of the Guomindang, and contributed to its demise.

Fluctuations in the Incidence of Corruption

In December 1951, corruption was rampant enough to prompt the government to launch the Three-Anti Campaign against corruption, waste, and bureaucratism. The Communists took over political control in 1949, but they could not change overnight conditions that gave rise to widespread corruption. The majority of those who had worked under the Guomindang remained with the new government. Since corruption permeated every level of the civil service in the late Republican era, many of those asked to stay were probably party to such practices. They might exercise more caution with their new employer but were unlikely to stop such activities completely. There were also those in the Communist ranks who were attracted to the illegal fallouts accessible to those holding positions of power.

Media reports focused on government success in fighting corruption. In a society that attached great importance to face or impression management, and with a young government so eager to show that everything was going smoothly, launching the anti-corruption campaign and releasing information on these cases were significant. *Renmin Ribao* reported 1,670 cases of corruption in twenty-seven central government bodies in December 1951.[6] Sichuan Province exposed fifteen thousand cases of corruption during the Three-Anti Campaign.[7] In the south-central region, about 45 percent of these cases involved skimming off public funds, withholding salaries from workers, embezzlement, conscripted labor, bribery, extortion, speculation, and other crimes reminiscent of the Republican period. The culprits were officials inherited from the previous era as well as draftees from among the war veterans or the recently recruited Communist Party members. Some of the high-profile criminals included the district party secretaries in Tianjin and the mayor of Wuhan and his two deputies.[8]

By the mid-fifties, the government seemed to have had corruption under control. Crime rate dropped from 93 per 100,000 in 1950 to 30 per 100,000 in 1956; the same number was reported in 1965.[9] In the United States, the rates were 786 per 100,000 and 1,434 per 100,000 in the corresponding years of 1956 and 1965.[10] This huge difference between the crime rates the two countries challenges the validity of attaching the same meaning to the Chinese figures as to those in the West. Chinese work and neighborhood organizations handled legal and administrative transgressions, investigated the accused, and punished the guilty. Only very serious cases reached the courts of law and appeared in official records. The official Chinese figures probably represented only a small fraction of such crimes.

The impression of a low crime rate, however, was confirmed by all my informants who lived in China during this period. Those old enough to remember looked back to the fifties with euphoria as the halcyon days of Communist rule. They recalled a party popular among the people, the officials as honest and clean. Some respondents, who had lived abroad in the forties only to return shortly after the establishment of the People's Republic to serve their country in various capacities, prided themselves as generally disciplined and dedicated, and were the first to *chiku* (taste bitterness). They claimed that a sense of mission and willingness to sacrifice pervaded the bureaucracy. Some informants went so far as to allege that "there was no corruption in the fifties." This idealistic picture was more likely an exaggeration romanticized with the passage of time. Incidence of legal and administrative corruption was certainly low but not absent simply because no society is perfect.

Some informants pointed to the sixties as the downturn in honest government and eagerly offered their explanation—state employees became disillusioned with the excesses of the political campaigns, such as the Anti-Rightist Movement, the Cultural Revolution, and others, when citizens were mobilized to expose and criticize others, thus splitting the local communities and undermining the officials' commitment to the socialist cause. Whatever the reasons behind the change, incidence of corruption remained low in the sixties and early seventies, even though it might have been higher than it was in the mid- and late fifties. In the early seventies, the crime rate averaged 50 per 100,000.[11] The *Siqing* (Four Cleans) Movement of 1962–1964 targeted corruption in the countryside. Account books, public granaries, collective properties, and work-point assessments were checked, but these investigations did not reveal large-scale transgressions.[12] Even during the Cultural Revolution, when investigation into any and every aspect of official behavior was fair play, accusations of bribery, extortion, embezzlement, fraud or other crimes associated with corruption were rare. Red Guards accused the officials not of black corruption but of administrative transgressions, such as indulging in cardplaying, using chauffeured cars, or eating good food —all cited as examples of bourgeois thinking.

Crime statistics were more available in the freer political climate of reform socialism. Between 1982 and 1985, the courts prosecuted 183,000 cases of economic crime, averaging 60,000 cases a year, and 224,000 individuals were found guilty. In 1988, the system handled 55,180 such cases. Because they were court cases, these cases would involve only *tanwu* and other property crimes stipulated in the criminal code and would not cover the less serious transgressions cited in the administrative code. Furthermore, these cases represented only 40 to 60 percent of all the cases accepted by the public prosecutor's office, which only prosecuted cases involving sums of over two thousand yuan.[13] This sum was readjusted to an even higher level in later years. There were private enterprises and self-employment in this period, and until the passing of the Company Law (*Gongxi Fa*) in 1994, there was no legal provision to prosecute corrupt employees in private businesses. This suggests that most, if not all, the guilty, averaging 72,000 per year, were state employees.[14] This would be about 0.8 percent of the 9.25 million civil servants in 1987,[15] much higher than the official number of 9,379 state employees found guilty of such crimes in 1988.[16]

Because crime statistics, like other statistics in China, are often used to demonstrate the success of government policies and agencies in fighting crimes, these statistics have all the fundamental methodological problems identified in criminology literature, and more.[17] Nevertheless, comparing the overall change in number of cases reported by the public security organs in this period (1976–1989) with the earlier one (1949–1976) would give a more meaningful picture of the fluctuation than relying on isolated statistics which might be using different yardsticks of measurement. At least, one is controlling for the problems inherent in these numbers coming from the same source. During reform socialism, the crime rate more than doubled rising from 30 per 100,000 in 1965 to 89 per 100,000 in 1981. It dropped to about 50 per 100,000 in the mideighties, and remained steady for a few years before experiencing another upturn. In 1988, the rate was 75 per 100,000; in 1989, it peaked at 181 per 100,000.[18]

From all accounts, by 1989 corruption had become a major social problem in Chinese society. Some informants charged that corruption was more widespread than during the Guomindang period; however, such charges are hard to authenticate with no comparable statistics from that era. I was especially suspicious when such comments were offered by those in their thirties and forties who were not old enough to have experienced or to remember Republican rule. But perhaps comparing current corruption with the hitherto worst period people knew was their way of expressing their frustration with what they perceived as a government lack of commitment and impotence to resolve the problem.

The government too recognized the seriousness of the problem. As early as 1982, the Central Committee of the Communist Party and the State Council in their April 13 Decision to Fight Economic Crimes admitted that economic crimes in the early eighties were more serious than those in 1952.[19] Since 1986, corruption was rated as the most serious social problem and it consistently replaced inflation as the number one complaint of citizens in different opinion polls.[20] In 1989, citizens' anger lent popular support to the students' demonstration against corruption on Tian'anmen Square, and the moral authority of the students' demands prevented the government, at least in the beginning, from dismissing their requests or peremptorily suppressing their movement. Overall, the evidence points to one conclusion: Legal and administrative corruption during reform socialism was more pervasive than during classical socialism.

Increased Values in Corrupt Exchanges

Some forms of corruption, such as embezzlement, are solo jobs; more often than not two parties are involved. When public property is being exchanged for private or public goods, one or both parties can be state officials. The state official uses, or to be more accurate misuses, the power entrusted in him/her to obtain public/private goods for personal benefits. The other party may do so willingly or unwillingly but they enter into the transaction because of what the power of the state official can procure.

Transactions in corruption have often been compared to exchanges in the marketplace; the goods traded, like those in the market, can be seen in the broadest economic sense as "bundles of satisfaction." Traders in corruption, like manufacturers in the market, are not just selling material goods but status, enjoyment, or a sense of satisfaction. Not all the currencies in these corrupt exchanges are tangible ones. Sometimes, the parties may get cash, material goods, services, and opportunities that make them happy, or they may be rewarded with honor or a sense of satisfaction.

Honor or face, in Chinese parlance, is a common denominator in many such exchanges. Honor, as I have suggested earlier, is so important in Chinese society that it can justify the repudiation of even close family members who bring shame to the family. State employees dispensed favors; threw large, sumptuous banquets; and built expensive offices and residences, often only to show off their own or their organization's power and influence. In return, they gained respect and honor, which they might or might not use as leverage to extract future favors. If they did, their clients would find it hard to turn down the requests of people in such influential and honorable positions. Honor is after all an indicator of power.

One cannot attach a price tag to honor. Honor, like confidence, is what others accord to the person, but it can be enhanced by material props. The people one knows, one's influence on other units, and the kinds of decisions one can make are all symbols of one's power. More tangible indicators are the number of one's staff, the size of one's budget, the banquets one gives, the vehicle one uses, the office building where one works, or one's office—the most visible of such symbols.

Even in the austere years of the early fifties, when the spending of public money was handled with caution, cadres tore down perfectly good buildings to build new and spacious ones that went beyond practical requirements, sometimes with enough floor capacity to accommodate twice the existing staff.[21] In 1953, the head of the market regulation society, who probably loved basketball, spent twenty million yuan to build an office building with an attached basketball court.[22] Reports of this nature largely disappeared in the sixties, only to reappear in the seventies, and the amount spent on these symbols of power escalated. Between 1974 and 1978, Liu Decai a party secretary in Dalian, allocated thirty-four million yuan for sixty-four buildings. These included an assembly hall to accommodate over one thousand people, twenty-one club houses, seven guest houses with three hundred beds, and two office buildings with floor space of over five thousand square meters each.[23] This kind of display of organizational power and affluence became even more pronounced in the materialistic climate of reform socialism. Units built dormitories, guest houses, and club houses for effect rather than to serve real needs. Even office buildings in remote areas like Ding'an Xian were ostentatiously decorated with colored tiles and stained glass windows and doors. One unit had an office building with 106 rooms and 2,100 square meters of floor space, averaging three rooms per staff member.[24] There were, of course, no budget lines to cover these kinds of expenses, and state employees contravened organizational guidelines by diverting money targeted for other purposes for these items. In return, they gained honor or face from their peers and subordinates.

If pursuing honor can be interpreted as self-aggrandizement, to misuse one's power to fulfill one's obligation to family and friends is a passive response to social pressure. Corruption prompted by such motivations nevertheless was common in China. Goodwill, or a sense of satisfaction in fulfilling one's obligation, was the reward officials obtained on these transactions. Like honor, it is another intangible commodity being exchanged in corrupt transactions and, again, the monetary value is hard to assess. Here, employees broke state regulations out of a sense of obligation to the recipients. Officials might owe their clients favors or, more often, they were related to them. The centrality of the family and the importance of interpersonal relationships in Chinese culture can explain the prevalence of nepotism motivated by a sense of obligation and goodwill. Chinese officials, like their compatriots, are committed to their family and other members of their social networks—the closer the member, the stronger the obligation, the more effort is expended. Some officials used their influence and broke administrative rules and even laws. In a socialist state, party membership is a prerequisite for upward mobility; and as a developing country, urban residence opens the door to more and better amenities. Consequently, those in high positions stretched administrative guidelines to recommend family members for membership in the party and for important offices, transferred relatives' household registration from the countryside to the cities, gave them city jobs, and secured housing or other comforts for them.[25] When the free market was introduced, officials provided their family members and friends with inside trading information, insured that they would be the first to get trading licenses, guaranteed them supplies and loans for their businesses and factories, and granted them export licenses so that they could benefit from these opportunities to make profits.[26] Even those in lowlier positions did what they could. Supervisors of granaries gave or lent their relatives grain; department store staff members gave their friends and relatives first choice of goods.[27]

The following case demonstrates the extent to which officials would go to look after their loved ones. The wife of the deputy head of the labor department decided to find a job after staying home for seventeen years. Her husband used his contacts at Luyang Milk Product Company and the Light Chemical Factory in Weian *Xian* to obtain documents certifying that she had worked in the first location from 1957 to 1961 and in the latter from 1962 to 1973. He then forged a work transfer document to get her a position in the light industries department. When she obtained only a temporary work permit, he deleted the word "temporary" and had her hired at Chu An Zhou Arts and Crafts Factory in 1974. Three years later, he used his prerogative as deputy head of the labor department to transfer her from a collective enterprise to a state job at the city's labor congress. Working for one's family is not a one-shot affair, but a long-term commitment. This department head used not only his direct power but also his influence to coerce others to commit fraud. Fulfilling obligations not only prompts breaking legal or organizational rules, but it is an integral part of a relationship involving reciprocity. In this case, the wife might not use the advantages of her public office to repay her husband, but in others the recipients owe the givers something and would be obliged to repay the favor if the need should arise. In a sense, the givers were banking credits that could be drawn upon in the future.

Because the Chinese work organizations are total institutions supplying their members' every need, the administrative staff not only provided salaries but also opportunities and services to the employees. They regulated their work conditions, marriage, housing, place of residence, number of children, childrens' education, and, indeed, almost all facets of the employees' existence. These decisions were valuable assets for corrupt officials; they capitalized on their positions as arbitrators in the distribution of state "goods" and traded the opportunities or services under their control to benefit their friends or get something in return from their clients. For example, an administrator could assign a married couple a quota to have a child and ask another couple to wait, or he/she could "overlook" an employee pregnant with a second baby so that she could try for a son. Or the administrator could give something more tangible. For example, a cadre raised the work points allotted for looking after the collective oxen from 90 to 210 points, allowing his friend, the new cowhand, to earn at least twice the income of her predecessor.[28] This cadre did not break any law; raising work points for a job was within his prerogative. But he clearly ignored the administrative guideline to avoid showing favoritism to family and friends. In the eighties, when officials gave their relatives or friends business licenses or export quotas, they essentially awarded them passports to wealth. The monetary impact of other decisions might be less direct or less obvious but equally if not more valuable. An authorization that allowed some children to attend a good school could open up favorable job opportunities that, in turn, would have tremendous impact on their future places of employment, housing, and other desirable benefits.

In the planned economy of China, where supplies are scarce and difficult to get, material goods are a common payment for favors. The operation of Wang Shaoxin, a real "professional" in bribery and gift giving made famous by Liu Bingyan in his article "Between Man and Demon" clearly demonstrates the important roles played by corrupt dealing in material goods and personal opportunities in a socialist economy. Wang was the manager and party secretary of a fuel company before being promoted to assistant director of the commerce department of Heilongjiang. She bribed her clients with materials and opportunities. Through her expert management of gift giving, she became one of the most powerful political figures in her region. Her "entertainment" budget between 1972 and 1978 was sixty-six thousand yuan. She kept a pig farm, three hundred *mu* of farmland, an agricultural by-product team, a fishing team, and a cold storage locker from which she could produce a constant supply of gifts for her "business" partners. When she was indicted in 1978, she had given out 8,700 *jin* of meat, fifty-nine pigs, 3,800 cartons of cigarettes, oil, one thousand *jin* of eggs, sixty thousand *jin* of grain, 8,900 *jin* of fish, vegetables, and 8,400 bottles of wine. In 1975, she created an education center to help youth in the rural areas join the military, pursue higher education, or learn technical skills needed in the urban areas; the beneficiaries were mostly children of state employees strategically located to help her or her unit and who wanted their children to return to the cities. By giving out gifts and opportunities, Wang created a network of friendly and powerful cadres beholden to her and willing to work in her interest. She became so influential that a report from the *xian* (county) disciplinary committee exposing her fell into her hands and was shelved. When she was finally brought to justice, 153 party members from seventy-one units were implicated.[29]

Newspaper reports at the time suggested that officials received more gifts and gifts of greater value over the years. In the classical socialist era, cadres were criticized for receiving wine, food, utensils, clothing materials, and other daily necessities and comforts from their clients.[30] They were bribed with a forty-yuan (U.S.$20) meal, a fountain pen, or some rare Chinese medicine like tiger bone.[31] In the eighties, gift giving proliferated. A survey in Yizhang *Xian* estimated that its population spent nine million yuan on gifts in the first six months of 1986, averaging sixty yuan a year for every family.[32] Another survey carried out six years later documented annual gift giving per family at 118 yuan.[33] Not all the gifts were bribes, but some bribes did pass as presents to the officials on festive occasions such as spring celebration or on special occasions such as their birthdays, childrens' weddings, christening, and housewarming. In the eighties, it was common knowledge that state companies set aside budgets especially for this purpose—a district commissioner inspecting local businesses was given nineteen banquets and twenty-five gifts worth 5,336 yuan in two months.[34] In the 1980 construction of the Baoshan Steel Mill, a white elephant investment outside Shanghai, local rumors had it that Chinese representatives were encouraged to sign the contract in return for the cadillacs "left behind" by the Japanese negotiators for their use. While gifts of smaller value were common, dishonest state employees often got large consumer items during the reform socialist period.

In addition to "gifts" from public or private sources, dishonest officials also helped themselves to state property while performing their duties, a practice condemned in the administrative codes. In 1953, a party secretary of the Zhizhong seventh district was reprimanded for taking twenty *jin* of fish from the villagers.[35] Another manager and accountant was punished for taking four hundred catty of salt, forty furlong of cloth, eighty *jin* of green hemp, four barrels, four pots, and hatchets.[36] By the sixties, a cadre was criticized for picking a few peanuts from the collective plot, and another working in a department store was chided for giving her child a candy.[37] In the reform socialist period, the value of the goods rose.

A good indicator is the cost of banquets in official circles. In the fifties, a Sichuan newspaper warned that if each organization spent an average of a hundred yuan a year for this purpose, several hundred thousand yuan would be wasted.[38] This amount was minuscule compared with the millions spent in the eighties, when a banquet could cost thousands of yuan.[39] On one occasion, a textile company spent nine thousand yuan on ten tables of food in addition to a few hundred bottles of wine and one thousand packs of cigarettes.[40] In 1987, China Advertising Company spent four hundred thousand yuan on entertaining in three days.[41] And these were not rare occasions. Authorities in Canton organized 219 banquets in a year. In total, one source estimated that between twenty-five and thirty billion yuan was spent on banquets in 1988.[42]

In most countries money is a popular medium of exchange in corruption because it is versatile, hard to trace, readily transferable, and can be easily changed into the goods one desires. Ever since the Communist government institutionalized central planning in the economy in the early fifties, the attractiveness of money was much attenuated because of its limited liquidity. Private ownership was condemned, goods were in scarce supply, and their distribution was state-controlled; therefore, money might not buy what one wanted. Furthermore, an ostentatious display of wealth might lead to unwanted attention and criticism. This situation changed in the eighties when it became once more acceptable to enjoy material comforts. Department stores carried a greater supply and variety of goods, patrons could buy large consumer items, including houses (not land), and money could be deposited in the bank with fewer questions asked. As a result, the value of money rose and with it its importance as a means of exchange in corruption.

In the first two years of Communist rule, when the market was still strong and money could buy what one wanted, bribery and embezzlement were frequently reported in the papers. In 1952, a Tianjin official skimmed off five million yuan from workers building airports, three million yuan from those engaged in flood prevention, and reaped a profit of twenty-two million yuan from the grain meant for the workers.[43] Such media reports fell sharply in the mid-fifties. In 1955, Fenghua in Anhui Province reported forty-two embezzlement cases in which the state lost twelve thousand yuan. Between March and December 1957, Taiyuan reported 139 cases involving forty-two thousand yuan, again averaging about three hundred yuan in each case. The cases reported in Sichuan about the same time involved similar amounts ranging from a hundred to five hundred yuan, the largest being 1,237 yuan.[44] In the mid-seventies, Wang Shouxin, who embezzled half a million yuan over eight years, shocked the public. But in 1987, a lowly bank officer made away with the same amount in only eight months.[45] In the same year, a unit head distributing construction materials made 166,000 yuan, or close to a third of that amount, in one transaction by charging the market rate instead of the lower state price.[46] The trend toward greater embezzlement in the reform socialist period is best illustrated by the case of Zhang Shiyan, a lowly administrative cadre in the seafood collection station. He embezzled eleven thousand yuan between 1971 and 1975, but in the following three years he got away with 226,762 yuan and tickets* worth 4,361 *jin* of grain.[47]

By the late eighties, embezzlement and fraud were so common that newspapers reported only cases involving thousands and millions of yuan; in the special economic zones, some public security bureaus would investigate and prosecute only cases above twenty thousand yuan. Moreover, bribery in the eighties took on the aspect of extortion. Government departments charged extra fees for routine services. Water works departments imposed special payments for power lines they had to put in, telephone companies asked for payment for prompt service, and the power company levied surcharges for doing its job. In Shandong, clients had to deposit two thousand yuan for every ten thousand borrowed from the banks. By means of these and other surcharges, government units accumulated huge sums in illegitimate ways. The Tianjin Light Industry Department earned twenty-six million yuan from illicit payments in a year.[48]

All these reports can lead us to one conclusion—even when inflation was controlled, the value of the exchanges involved in

---

*Since the mid-fifties and until the late eighties, the Chinese government regulated grain consumption by issuing grain tickets specifying the amount that could be bought by each person. A person could make money by selling these tickets to peasants or illegal residents who could not otherwise buy such food products.

corruption was generally higher in the eighties than in the previous decades under Communist rule. The fact that the frequency and the value of these exchanges rose when the supply of goods, as well as the sources of these supplies, increased leads one to question the accepted wisdom of the linear relationship between corruption and the supply of goods, and that between pricing and the goods supplied in corruption.[49] Here the subjective valuation of money and material goods seemed to be more important—a perspective which we shall examine in the next chapter.

Changing Forms of Corruption

Corruption was as rampant in the first three years of Communist rule as it had been in the Republican period. Dishonest officials used opportunities offered in the course of performing their duties to cheat the government of its resources. They embezzled public funds, even took for themselves disaster relief meant for the victims. They misappropriated state property and used it for their own enjoyment. When purchasing materials for the state, they collaborated with merchants in forging receipts for higher amounts than those paid out. Sometimes they went into partnership with these businessmen, using their information on supplies in different places to buy goods at low prices and resell them at times or locations when and where the prices rose. They acted like overlords toward the public, collecting more grain from the peasants than that stipulated by the center; forcing people into private labor service to build, for example, their own residences; and demanding gifts and services from those under their charge, with the latter expecting nothing in return except perhaps freedom from harassment.[50] When they bought grain from the peasants on the state's behalf, they often negotiated and forced a lower price and pocketed the difference. In one extreme case, rural cadres even forced their own useless currencies on peasants selling them grain.[51]

By the mid-fifties, these blatant abuses gave way to more subtle misuse of power, or the gray corruption characteristic of the socialist system discussed in chapter 3. The markets had disappeared, the rules governing speculation were stricter, and occurrences of this nature dropped. In 1962, the associate chairman of Henan's Fanzi Commune was accused of aiding speculation even for selling sixty brooms to a relative, who without her knowledge, later sold them in his home village at seventeen yuan profit each.[52] Reports of bribery and extortion were rare; since the values of the items involved were small, these blatant abuses probably blended into the Chinese tradition of gift giving and became less serious and more difficult to detect or prosecute. Instead of exploiting those under their control, who now had few private possessions, cadres exploited state property usually in the course of their official duties. They enjoyed and wasted state resources on the job. They engaged in false reporting to get more materials from the state or to gain greater honor for themselves and their organizations. They kept material resources from their superiors, and hoarded or bartered them for other necessities for later production use. Black corruption had turned gray.

In the eighties, the incidence of every type of corruption rose. Reports of extortion and the embezzlement of state subsidies, and relief funds reappeared.[53] With fiscal decentralization and more money available at the lower levels, there were more cases of bribery and wastage of state resources. The most interesting development was the reemergence of speculation, smuggling, consumer fraud, kickbacks, and tax abuse—the types of corruption characteristic of unbridled capitalism and reminiscent of the early fifties.[54]

With the return of the market, state officials like those in the early fifties once more collaborated with private businesses to make their personal fortunes; by 1988, 47,900 cadres were involved in 477,000 such companies across the nation.[55] This social group also used their official positions to take advantage of the new business opportunities in other ways. They bullied the private business sectors and were in an even stronger position to do so than their official counterparts in the early fifties. In the early fifties, merchants relied on state officials mainly for licenses and information on supply and demand; however the newly emergent group of merchants needed, in addition, authorizations for employment quotas, export licenses, import permits, and the supply of many state goods. The dishonest officials used their power to authorize permits and their access to state property as capital. In 1989, a cadre of the Huhehot labor department made 33,650 yuan in this way; in another case, thirteen approval notices were sold for half a million yuan.[56] When the profit came in, the merchants were to return a portion as tax to the state, but the amounts imposed were often arbitrary, subject to the goodwill of the tax collectors. Many underreported their profit or bribed the tax collectors to get lower assessments.[57] And when the business proved profitable, local officials even forced themselves on the entrepreneurs as partners.

The ability to retain some of the profits encouraged many state factories to produce more goods and goods tailored to the consumers' tastes. Their profits, however, sometimes came from cost cutting which compromised quality. In the first few years of Communist rule, companies eager to make a profit substituted substandard goods and, in some of the worst cases, even poisoned their customers by mixing tung oil with cooking oil.[58] The sale of ersatz goods largely disappeared in the late fifties and sixties only to reappear in the reform socialist period. In the eighties, some state-run stores again tampered with their stocks. Water was added to milk; wool was sprinkled with lead, iron, and glass filings to increase its weight; 0.91 *jin* of vinegar was sold as one *jin;* and part of a measuring rod was cut off to give the customer less cloth.[59] Manufacturers recycled used bicycles and passed them off as the popular Flying Pigeon brand; others made low-grade cosmetics and labeled them Swan or Double Celebration products.[60] These consumer frauds were perpetrated not only by fly-by-night operators but by state and collective enterprises, such as when fifty collective enterprises in Fujian produced substandard medicine.[61] Even in the eighties, state factories were supposed to supply the state procurement first, then they could sell their above-quota output in the open market. Instead, some kept their products from the state by not declaring their total production and siphoned the products left behind to sell in the free market. In 1983, the center collected 890,000 tons less steel than was stipulated in the central plan; yet

330,000 tons were available in the market. Since steel manufacturing is capital intensive and produced by state plants, this suggests that the managers of these plants withheld their output to sell for profit. The same thing happened in the cement industry. *Renmin Ribao* reported that cement collection was 4.7 million tons below the state target and yet there were 0.88 million tons available at the higher market price.[62] Selling state goods in the open market brought millions to those involved. Speculation became rampant. Sometimes goods were sold and resold. Profits were made without the goods ever leaving the warehouses. As a result of this process, the price of the same set of steel plates rose from 1,750 yuan to 4,600 yuan per ton after 129 transactions, and the price of aluminum jumped from six thousand yuan to fourteen thousand yuan per ton in a year.[63]

If we ignore the aberrations of the first three years, and treat the years 1949 to 1989 as composed of two distinct periods, we find corruption in the classical socialist period different from corruption in the reform socialist period. In the earlier period, state property was the major target of illegitimate activities, which often benefited both the individual and the organization. The beneficiaries did not necessarily take the property for their private use, but used their ill-gotten gains on the job. Reflecting the traditional culture, personal relationships were important in determining how opportunities or other conveniences would be awarded to clients. In the reform socialist era, corruption became more complex. Not only was there gray corruption characteristic of socialism, but new forms of corruption reminiscent of those in nascent capitalism emerged. State property was still a major target, but private property became more important. Unethical managers of economic units defrauded the government, underreporting the volume of their business and evading tax; they cheated their clients who more and more were coming from the private sector by delivering substandard products and raising prices. Dishonest state officials, enjoying illegitimate users' rights, increasingly tended to appropriate state and private property. Personal relationships were still an important consideration in these transactions, but many exchanges had become more like the impersonal free market exchanges where money was the major consideration.

Widening Network

If the market is a network of social exchanges that binds the economy together, corruption can also be viewed as a network of interpersonal interactions in the illegal or second economy.[64] At the individual level, bribery or extortion involves a state official and his/her client who may also be a state employee. At the organizational level, units link vertically with echelons below and above them, and also forward and backward in their horizontal relationships; they cultivate good relations through legitimate and illegitimate means with other echelons or units to ensure timely help when needed. As the incidence of corruption grows, it is only logical that the number of persons (whether they are representing their own interests or those of their organizations) involved will also increase. Moreover, when the property at issue increases in value, there is also likely to be greater cooperation among a larger number of accomplices.

In the sixties and seventies in China, agents of the production or marketing units wined and dined the representatives of supplier or buyer units and gave them free samples or products at below costs. In the eighties, these forms of extortion or bribery multiplied.[65] In the past, factory managers mainly had to keep their suppliers happy; now they had to please representatives from the licensing board, the power company, the water works, the telephone services, public security, the railroad company, and any other units whose services they would need in their everyday operations.[66] A manager of a small Shanghai lock factory explained the difficulties of doing business. Besides its suppliers, the factory management had to please the neighborhood policeman so that access to the premises would not be blocked and delivery trucks could stop at the front entrance. They had to be on good terms with representatives of the neighborhood committee so that the latter would not complain when the trucks did stop at the front gate. They had to please the health and fire inspectors because these officers could easily halt production for minor violations. On top of that, they had to be friendly with the power department who could cut off their electricity for a few days, with the excuse of coping with the scarcity of energy in the city. If they needed to transport goods by train, they paid extra to the railway staff for freight space to have their products delivered on time. The suppliers of the classical socialist period were now replaced by a network of agents, or *guanxi hu* (relational households). To ensure smooth operation of their business, administrators had to please or bribe not one or two but a number of different clients.

With the principle of reciprocity at work in corruption, as in almost all social relations, the increased number and forms of such misdemeanors in the eighties could only generate a momentum that exponentially widened the circle of participants and increased the practice of corruption. In the example given earlier, the deputy head of the labor department was indebted to at least the two administrative personnel who provided the forged records of his wife's employment; therefore, it would be difficult for him to refuse their reasonable or unreasonable requests in the future. When it came to nepotism, officials ignored organizational rules and regulations; they often suspended all moral judgment particularly when their children were involved. They secured them prestigious schools, good jobs, and spacious accommodations. They shielded their children from the law; defended them even if they were guilty of rape, embezzlement, or theft; provided them refuge or hid them if they were being pursued by public security; and, if they got caught, protected them from prosecution and punishment.[67]

Working for their family in this way was so common that high-level officials developed informal networks in the process. In its mildest form, officials gave their colleagues' children jobs in their departments, household transfers, or other such desirable goods; they, of course, would expect the favor to be returned for their sons and daughters when the time came. This way of banking credits made nepotism and other such forms of corruption subtle and less easily detectable unless operational rules were blatantly violated, such as when the candidates receiving the entitlements clearly were not qualified. But there is ambiguity even in the most clearly delineated regulation which provided cadres room to maneuver. Moreover, these reciprocal favors expanded the number of people involved in corruption in the long run and tied them to a closely knit group.

The previous examples of organizational bribery, extortion, and other forms of corruption show that often corruption is a collaborative project. At the very least, the giver and the recipient are sealed in a culture of silence. As the scale and the value of these operations increased in the eighties, more people were involved—especially obvious were cases of speculation and smuggling which involved at least two geographic locations (the place of origin and the destination). Moreover, the division of functions in bureaucratic organizations generally inhibits the same person from putting together all the requisites to carry out a corrupt operation. Units with the resources may not have the transportation facilities, and those with the means of transportation may not have the outlets. In the early fifties, speculators had to bribe state officials to sell them goods and bribe transportation units to bring the products to the sale site. In the famous smuggling case mentioned earlier, even a powerful cadre like the mayor of Wuhan had to collaborate with the party secretary of Tianjin. In another incident, even the military was involved, providing transportation, military uniforms, arms, and documents to move the merchandise.[68]

In the eighties, as the value and volume of smuggled goods increased, so did the number of participants. The smuggling operation on Hainan Island, strategically located on the southeast coast, shows the extent of such involvement. According to the "Report on Hainan Island Import of Cars and Other Luxury Goods," local officials illegally imported 89,000 cars, 2.86 million television sets, 252,000 video cassette recorders, and 122,000 motorcycles in the fifteen months between January 1984 and March 1985; and then they shipped the goods to other parts of the country where they commanded prices five to six times their cost. Eighty-eight of the ninety-four local government departments were involved. Military

and public security officials were indicted for delivering the contraband—the military used its boats and other facilities for transportation, and public security provided the special license
exempting the convoys from inspection.[69] In addition, there were
members of the naval police and the customs who turned a blind
eye to bulky items like 89,999 motor cars; people in the finance
department who provided them foreign currency, most likely illegally, to buy these goods or at least to make the downpayments in
Hong Kong; purchasing agents who bought the huge quantity of
supplies; and agents on location to distribute the goods and find
buyers. In turn, the buyers had to obtain the cash, most likely
illegally, to buy the contraband; since the buyers, and especially
those getting motor vehicles, had to be representatives of state
units that could afford such items, more collusion and regulation
breaking had to occur to get the money and to cover up the illegal
source of the goods. The smuggling of cars and other commodities was common on the east coast of China; this is only one of
the most famous cases. The scale of this operation and other
lesser ones suggest that such activities had to be carefully orches-
trated by strategically located top people in the different government branches, who had the personnel and material resources at
their disposal.[70] These players, each in their own way breaking
legal or administrative codes, would cover for each other. The
resulting collusion or cooperation could only contribute to the
culture of silence and what the Chinese authorities called *baohu
shan,* or protective umbrella.

Subordinates within these work units were drawn willingly or
unwillingly into the role of accomplices. As they performed their
duties on orders from above, they must have been aware to some
extent of such goings-on even though they may not have been
formally apprised of the situation. But employees remained silent
perhaps out of habituation to obeying and accepting authority.
Ole Bruun noted that even the entrepreneurial private business
people never questioned their rights and silently complied with
government officials' demands.[71] For those employed within the
work units, the pressure to comply would be greater. But the

pressure did not spring from these employees' concern for their job security, because they had lifetime appointment, at least under the socialist period we are looking at. They did it more likely for fear of retaliation from their supervisors or ostracism by their peers, which would be equally hard to take because they usually remained in the same organization for life. There was an additional reason to remain silent in the eighties. As authority was decentralized to the lower levels, unit heads had more resources to distribute to the employees and the latter became more dependent on the organization; the reach of the state in the form of the hold of the immediate supervisors over their staff increased.[72]

When government departments instituted *xinfang,* the practice of civilians' reporting any official irregularities anonymously, some unit managers intentionally or unintentionally bought off the workers. Because illegal business practices brought extra income to the organization, part of the returns were distributed to the members in the form of bonuses, small consumer items, food, and better fringe benefits. Even in the case of the textile factory mentioned earlier, where over nine thousand yuan was spent on a banquet for the top administrative staff, lower ranking employees and workers were given a meal at a cheaper restaurant close by and told not to tell.[73] The success of corruption requires a vertical as well as a lateral network of silence. In cases where units wanted to defraud their superiors, they had to buy off their subordinates. In so doing, those engaged in corruption developed not just a protective umbrella shading themselves from above but a box behind whose walls they and the increasing number of people involved could hide from those beside, above, and below them. Those involved in corruption may not have taken an oath of silence, but they were nevertheless as tight-lipped about these occurrences.

An Overview

Between 1949 and 1989, changes in the incidence of corruption, the overall monetary value, the complexity, and the number of participants involved could perhaps be best represented by a parabolic curve. The initial point of the graph is quite high for 1949, then the line dips rapidly in the late fifties to a low point in the sixties, only to rise again in the seventies; the final point in 1989 is higher than the initial one.

Corruption in China in the early fifties was like that in many developing societies with market economies: Society was still in the grips of the traditional culture, social relationships were personalized, the power of state officials was strong, and outside supervision was weak. Corrupt practices were widespread, nepotism was common, and state officials collaborated with the private sector to defraud state and individual property. From the mid-fifties to the late seventies, the number of and the monetary value involved in corruption cases dropped. Corrupt practices resembled more closely those in other socialist countries: Officials targeted mostly state, and not private, property. Moreover, they preferred material goods to cash, enjoyed illegitimate benefits and conveniences on the job but did not embezzle state property, and broke laws and regulations to benefit both themselves and their organizations. In the reform socialist period, gray corruption, popular under classical socialism, proliferated with the number of occurrences and the monetary values of these cases surpassing those of the early fifties. With the reintroduction of the market and expanded forms of private ownership, corrupt practices found in nascent capitalist societies emerged—once more, money became important and these transactions resembled the impersonal market exchanges in the West. Corruption in the eighties took on the characteristics of both the socialist and capitalist societies.

Notes

1. Lucien Bianco, *Origins of the Chinese Revolution, 1914–1949* (Stanford: Stanford University Press, 1971), p. 118.
2. Suzanne Pepper, *Civil War in China: The Political Struggle, 1945–1949* (Berkeley: University of California Press, 1978), pp. 24, 28, 150, 152.
3. Lloyd Eastman, *Seeds of Destruction: Nationalist China in War and Revolution, 1937–1949* (Stanford: Stanford University Press, 1984), p. 65; Bianco, *Origins.* p. 101; Helen Siu, *Agents and Victims in South China: Accomplices in Rural Revolution* (New Haven: Yale University Press, 1989), pp. 75–76.
4. Bianco, *Origins,* pp. 101, 110.

5. Eastman, *Seeds of Destruction*, pp. 62, 152, 204–5.

6. A. Doak Barnett, *Communist China: The Early Years, 1949–1955* (New York: Praeger, 1965), p. 138.

7. *Sichuan Ribao,* February 13, 1953, p. 1.

8. A. Doak Barnett, *Chinese Communist Politics in Action* (Seattle: University of Washington Press, 1969), p. 244; Chen Nai-chao, *Zhonggong Tanwu Jiantao* (An examination of corruption in Communist China) (Hong Kong: Xia Shiji Cubanshe, 1953), p. 6; Gong Ting, *The Politics of Corruption in Contemporary China* (Westport, Conn.: Praeger, 1994), p. 61.

9. He Bingsong, "Crime and Control in China," in *Crime and Control in Comparative Perspective,* ed. Hans-Gunther Heiland, Louis I. Shelley, and Hisao Katoh, pp. 241–59 (New York: Walter de Gruyter, 1992).

10. *Statistical Abstract of the United States, 1957,* p. 139; *Statistical Abstract of the United States, 1967,* p. 149.

11. He Bingsong, "Crime and Control," p. 244.

12. Richard Madsen, *Morality and Power in a Chinese Village* (Berkeley: University of California Press, 1984), chapter 3.

13. *Law and Politics Tribune* 5 (1989): 37–45, cited in Jean Louis Rocca, "Corruption and Its Shadow: An Anthropological View of Corruption in China," *China Quarterly,* no. 130 (June 1992): 402–16.

14. "People's Republic of China Communist Party Standing Committee Report, 30 May 1986," reported in *People's Republic of China People's Supreme Court Annual Report, 1986,* p. 68.

15. *Fubai: Huobi Yu Quanli de Jiaohuan,* (Corruption: An exchange of money and power) (Beijing: Zhongguo Zhanwang Chubanshe, 1989), p. 39.

16. *Nianzheng Jianshe Shouce* (Handbook to build an honest governance), (Chengdu: Sichuan Renmin Chubanshe, 1980), p. 115.

17. A.D. Biderman and J.P. Lynch, *Understanding Crime Incidence Statistics: Why the UCR Diverges from the NCS* (New York: Springer-Verlag, 1991); Robert O'Brien, *Crime and Victimization Data* (Beverly Hills: Sage, 1985); Doris Layton MacKenzie, Phyllis T. Baunach, and Roy R. Roberg, *Measuring Crime Large Scale, Long Range Efforts* (Albany: State University of New York Press, 1990).

18. *People's Republic of China People's Supreme Court Annual Report, 1987* and *1988.* He Bingsong, "Crime and Control," p. 245; Dean Rojek, "Changing Directions of Chinese Social Control," in *Comparative Criminal Justice,* ed. Charles B. Field and Richter H. Moore, Jr., *Traditional and Nontraditional Systems of Law and Control* (Prospect Heights, Ill.: Waveland Press, 1996), p. 241.

19. *Cha chu guandao anjian shiyong fa lü shouce* (A practical handbook in investigating cases of speculation) (Beijing: Falü Chubanshe, 1989), p. 21.

20. SWB FE 8351, August 30, 1986, quoted in Clemens Stubbe Ostergaard and Christina Petersen, "Official Profiteering and the Tiananmen Square Demonstrations in China," *Corruption and Reform* 6 (1991): 87–107; Gong Ting, *Politics of Corruption,* p. 135.

21. *Sichuan Ribao,* September 4, 1952, p. 4; January 5, 1953, p. 1; March 1, 1953, p. 3; April 30, 1953, p. 2.

22. *Sichuan Ribao,* March 1, 1953, p. 3.

23. *Renmin Ribao,* April 6, 1978, p. 1; April 17, 1978, p. 1.

24. *Renmin Ribao,* January 13, 1979, p. 2.

25. *Renmin Ribao,* April 9, 1980, p. 3; October 12, 1980, p. 1; December 18, 1983, p. 5; March 17, 1984, p. 5; January 25, 1986, p. 5.

26. *Renmin Ribao,* July 18, 1980, p. 4; *Sichuan Ribao,* February 24, 1953, p. 2; Gao Gang, *Fandui Tanwu Tuihua, Fendui Guanliao Zhuyi* (Oppose the acceleration of corruption, oppose bureaucratism) (Guangzhou: Huanan Renmin Chubanshe, 1952), p. 3.

27. *Sichuan Ribao,* July 27, 1963, p. 2; March 1, 1970, p. 1; June 23, 1984, p. 5.

28. *Sichuan Ribao,* December 8, 1964, p. 1.

29. *Renmin Ribao,* April 23, 1979, p. 2; October 25, 1979, p. 4; February 29, 1980, p. 1; April 1, 1980, p. 1.

30. *Renmin Ribao,* November 5, 1983, p. 5.

31. *Sichuan Ribao,* October 14, 1957, p. 2.

32. *Renmin Ribao,* November 26, 1986, p. 4.

33. *China Times Weekly,* September 27, 1992, p. 70, cited in Gong Ting, *Politics of Corruption,* p. 127.

34. *Renmin Ribao,* June 2, 1989, reported in Gong Ting, *Politics of Corruption,* 1994, p. 127.

35. *Sichuan Ribao,* February 21, 1953, p. 1; February 24, 1953, p. 2.

36. *Sichuan Ribao,* December 3, 1952, p. 2.

37. *Sichuan Ribao,* December 25, 1964, p. 2; May 21, 1975, p. 2.

38. *Sichuan Ribao,* August 11, 1955, p. 2.

39. *Renmin Ribao,* October 31, 1980, p. 4; September 2, 1981, p. 3; December 27, 1981, p. 4; February 13, 1982, p. 5; December 1, 1983, p. 7; December 14, 1983, p. 2; December 2, 1988, p. 1; December 7, 1988, p. 5.

40. *Renmin Ribao,* March 19, 1988, p. 5.

41. *Renmin Ribao,* August 15, 1987, pp. 1, 5.

42. Rocca, "Corruption and Its Shadow," pp. 402–16.

43. Chen Nai-chao, *Zhonggong Tanwu Jiantao,* p. 6.

44. *Anhui Ribao,* July 24, 1956, p. 3; *Shaanxi Ribao,* January 12, 1958, p. 3; *Sichuan Ribao,* August 22, 1957, p. 2; August 7, 1958, p. 3.

45. *Renmin Ribao,* December 3, 1988, p. 1. The bank employee embezzled 570,000 yuan in eight months.

46. *Renmin Ribao,* November 18, 1981, p. 3; June 24, 1982, p. 1.

47. *Renmin Ribao,* October 11, 1980, p. 3.

48. *Renmin Ribao,* July 8, 1983, p. 1; December 24, 1984, p. 2; July 24, 1987, p. 2; August 17, 1987, p. 1.

49. Robert O. Tilman, "Emergence of Black-Market Bureaucracy, Administration, and Corruption in the New States," *Public Administration Review* 28, no. 5 (September/October 1968): 440–42.

50. *Sichuan Ribao,* March 28, 1953, p. 3.

51. *Sichuan Ribao,* December 31, 1954, p. 2.

52. *Renmin Ribao,* July 21, 1984, p. 5.

53. Rocca, "Corruption and Its Shadow."

54. Peter Harris, "Socialist Graft: The Soviet Union and the People's Re-

public of China—A Preliminary Survey," *Corruption and Reform* 1 (1986): 13–32.

55. *Renmin Ribao,* August 30, 1989, July 7, 1990, quoted in Gong Tong, *Politics of Corruption,* p. 130.

56. *Wen Hui Bao,* June 23, 1989, and *Renmin Ribao,* November 22, 1988, quoted in Gong Ting, *Politics of Corruption,* p. 132. See also Rocca, "Corruption and Its Shadow."

57. Ole Bruun, *Business and Bureaucracy in a Chinese City: An Ethnography of Private Business Households in Contemporary China* (Berkeley: University of California Institute of Asian Studies, 1993), chapter 5; Peter Harris, "Socialist Graft: The Soviet Union and the People's Republic of China: A Preliminary Survey," p. 27.

58. *Sichuan Ribao,* February 17, 1953, p. 1; August 6, 1953, p. 3.

59. *Renmin Ribao,* October 8, 1979, p. 3; July 9, 1987, p. 3; February 14, 1988, p. 1; October 22, 1988, p. 2.

60. *Renmin Ribao,* June 12, 1980, p. 2; December 15, 1980, p. 3; December 26, 1981, p. 5; March 26, 1982, p. 2; February 5, 1983, p. 2; August 10, 1983, p. 2; August 2, 1984, p. 7; September 28, 1984, p. 5; March 4, 1987, p. 5; June 18, 1987, p. 5; June 21, 1987, p. 2; July 9, 1987, p. 2; September 11, 1987, p. 2; December 19, 1987, p. 5; Febbruary 14, 1988, p. 1; October 20, 1988, p. 2.

61. *People's Republic of China People's Supreme Court Report, 1987.*

62. *Renmin Ribao,* July 21, 1983, p. 1.

63. *Renmin Ribao,* June 22, 1988; July 21, 1989 quoted in Gong Ting, *Politics of Corruption,* p. 132.

64. Cyril S. Belshaw, *Traditional Exchange and Modern Markets* (Englewood Cliffs, N.J.: Prentice Hall, 1965), p. 75.

65. *Renmin Ribao,* October 31, 1980, p. 4; September 23, 1981, p. 4; October 25, 1981, p. 5; December 27, 1981, p. 4; December 1, 1983, p. 7; December 14, 1983, p. 2; June 15, 1984, p. 2; June 17, 1984, p. 1; August 18, 1987, p. 1; November 17, 1988, p. 1.

66. *Renmin Ribao,* February 23, 1984, p. 1; March 30, 1984, p. 4; December 26, 1986, p. 2; July 18, 1987, p. 3; May 20, 1988, p. 1.

67. *Renmin Ribao,* June 20, 1980, p. 2; October 28, 1980, p. 4; September 18, 1983, p. 4.

68. Chen Nai-chao, *Zhonggong Tanwu Jiantao,* p. 49.

69. *Dongxi* (East-West) 4:1, No. 36 (1986): 85–87; *Tsangming* 9, no. 9 (1985): 33–36; *Nineties* (June 1985): 52–54.

70. In another case, the managers of Shenjiang naval yard bought a dilapidated merchant ship at 760,000 yuan and sold it for 1.78 million yuan after bribing twenty-five officials and party members, including the director of the Port Authority, two engineers, and the chief technician of the Wenzhou maritime transport company. *Fazhi Ribao,* August 2, 1989, p. 1, cited in Rocca, "Corruption and Its Shadow," pp. 406–7.

71. Bruun, *Business and Bureaucracy,* p. 120.

72. Gong Ting, *Politics of Corruption,* p. 125; Vivienne Shue, *The Reach of the State* (Stanford: Stanford University Press, 1988).

73. *Renmin Ribao,* March 19, 1988, p. 5.

5

The Dynamics of Corruption

What caused the fluctuations in corruption in socialist China? The task of finding an answer to this question is not a simple one. Corruption is a complex concept that has many different aspects. In some cases, dishonest officials dealt in public property, in other cases, in private property. Sometimes, state employees defrauded their superiors or their own organizations, and at other times their subordinates. Sometimes, their actions involved subterfuges and cover-ups; at other times, they were outright exercises of power or sheer exploitation. Sometimes, the corruption benefited their organizations, and at other times themselves. The challenge here is to find a comprehensive explanation for variations in these phenomena.

Asking a Different Question

Current explanations of corruption in socialist societies come from diverse disciplinary perspectives. I shall focus on those perspectives most pertinent to explaining the situation in regard to corruption in China. The economic approach primarily views the commerce of corruption as a second economy. Econometric analyses are used to demonstrate how bribery is beneficial to the circulation of goods, the assumption being that the centralization of power and resources in the hands of state bureaucrats results in inefficiencies, bottlenecks, and inadequate supplies. Through bribery, resourceful citizens can facilitate the circulation of goods, reduce the time of queuing, redistribute scarce goods, redirect money from consumption to investment, and introduce an element of competition.[1] Corruption is a response to the pressures of shortage economy. Jean Oi, coming from a political science perspective, focuses on the position of the team-level cadres wedged between the demands of the supervisors and the claims of their subordinates.[2] Beholden to both their superiors and inferiors in the discharge of their duties, these cadres engage in clientelism, bending rules, or other forms of patronage to relieve the pressures coming from these opposite directions. Peter Lee, another political scientist, examines the Chinese bureaucratic structures that gave rise to different types of corruption, drawing out the similarities with the Soviet Union.[3] More recently, Mayfair Yang, an anthropologist, has analyzed the traditional practice of gift giving—a behavior firmly anchored in Chinese tradition as a survival mechanism in a scarce economy. Under socialism, gift giving, or bribery, became a means for those positioned outside the locus of power to bypass the restrictions from above, resist oppression, and manifest resilience.[4]

Except for Oi's analysis of clientelism and Lee's comparative study, which broaden the forms of corruption studied, the focus in the literature is primarily on bribery. Zeroing in on bribery might be justifiable for some Eastern European socialist countries where it was widespread, but not so in China. My analysis suggests that it was not the dominant form of corruption in the first thirty years, though it is harder to be as definitive about the eighties. However, even then, increase in bribery was accompanied by a rise in speculation, tax evasion, and smuggling, which deserve equal attention and also need to be explained. Furthermore, bribery is not unique to socialist societies. Ronald Wraith and Edgar Simpkins have identified bribery as a serious problem in developing societies with a capitalist economic base, which leads one to believe that perhaps bribery may be a characteristic of developing rather than of socialist societies.[5] Thus, highlighting bribery in the study of corruption in socialist China may not be entirely justified.

Most of these social scientists have premised their explanations of corruption on a restrictive and inefficient economic system where officials and their clients have to use innovative solutions to resolve these problems. The centralization of power, the oppressiveness of higher authorities, the concentration of privileges, and inefficiency in the production and distribution of supplies prompted the resourceful, those deprived of opportunities, or those under pressure from different sides in an organization to indulge in illegal and illegitimate acts. The logic of these arguments is not in question; in chapter 3 I took a similar approach to show how Chinese socialist structures encouraged officials to take certain types of corrupt action that were either not found or less used in capitalist societies. But to do so is not the same as saying that these are the characteristics only of socialist societies or that socialist societies are more prone to corruption or more corrupt than capitalist societies. If one takes the latter position, then one is saying that the decentralization of power, a broader distribution of privileges, and greater efficiency in production and distribution of goods should lead to less corruption. But then, how to explain why corruption in China rose in the eighties, when such modifications were taking place in the more or less socialist political structures?

The fallacy of this approach becomes even more apparent when we examine a similar or parallel position adopted by some social scientists, mainly in socialist societies, to explain corruption under capitalism. They believe that the root causes of corruption in this case are the avarice, inequities, and exploitative structures of the capitalist system—that people are sometimes deprived even of bare necessities because of the inherent inequities found in a capitalist society. Because of the monopoly of power and the concentration of privileges among the bourgeoisie, people are forced to bribe officials and break rules in other ways to obtain desired goods. This explanation sounds familiar. Here, too, those outside the locus of power—and in this case the workers —are heroes resisting a flawed system. The corollaries following from this premise are: (1) once the socialist system is in place, corruption will disappear, and (2) if corruption is found in these socialist societies, it must be a residue of the feudal past or a by-product of the polluting influence of the West.[6] While not discounting these possibilities, Western social scientists would no doubt disagree with such a categorical conclusion. If one pushes the "corruption inherent to socialist societies" argument further, one would have come up with an equally simplistic explanation putting the blame on the socialist system, and romanticizing the perpetrators, forgetting that sometimes and especially in cases of corruption, perpetrators can be people in privileged power positions.

Both the capitalist and the socialist systems have organizational peculiarities that make them susceptible to certain forms of corruption. These systemic characteristics, however, only offer the backdrop for understanding corruption in these societies, but because they also offer only a static analytical framework, they cannot explain the dynamics of corruption over time. One has to look elsewhere to find the answer to why there have been fluctuations in corruption in China.

Corruption as a Social Act

In order to understand the fluctuations of corruption, one has to break it down into its basic units and understand how it operates at the individual level, before one can fully appreciate the effects of larger social forces on corruption. Corruption, while a social phenomenon and a public issue, is ultimately a number of interacting but discreet purposive social acts. Corruption, like other crimes, is the exercise of differential powers in a social situation with one party imposing his/her will on another. The powers, while always being exercised illegitimately on such occasions, may come from the perpetrators' physical strength, from control of certain resources, or from an otherwise legitimate source. For example, robbery is using physical force to obtain property belonging to another; and rape is the violation of another's body through the use of force. In corruption, the state employee, alone or in collaboration with others, seizes opportunities offered by his/her position to use trade, or steal public or private property for personal gain.

A bureaucracy or complex organization always has to delegate power to its incumbents to fulfill their responsibilities; consequently, the opportunities of state employees to abuse the authority vested in their public office are always there. The extent to which these incumbents will engage in corruption rests on motivations and constraints peculiar to the situation. The perception of the individual's needs and the extent to which he/she can "justifiably" break certain social norms and state regulations depend on that individual's moral position and personal philosophy. The former orientation provides the motivation for the action and the latter the constraints. The means used, and the kinds and value of the property, are different in each corrupt action; these are circumscribed by the nature of the real and perceived opportunities and by the type of constraints put on the individual. With other things being equal, the more diverse the access channels, the greater the opportunities to obtain the goods, and the slimmer the chance of detection, the more likely the individual will be to indulge in various types of corrupt activities. Few will argue with these basic sociological concepts.

Nevertheless, it is not my purpose to understand the particularistic situations that make certain individuals in a bureaucracy indulge in corrupt activities and others to abstain. Rather, my purpose is to understand why cohorts of state officials in different time periods tended to choose varying courses of action. Why did most eschew corruption, particularly smuggling and speculation, in the classical socialist period and engage in false reporting, bartering, and wastefulness instead? Why did more state officials turn to bribery, embezzlement, speculation, and other forms of corruption in the reform socialist era? Why did they demand higher returns from their corrupt activities in the eighties? Why did they go after private property in the reform socialist era and not in the classical socialist one? A comprehensive answer addressing all these questions will necessarily be abstract and general.

A study of this nature needs to be conducted on a relatively macro level of analysis. Running parallel to the individual's moral beliefs is the society's ideology or moral culture; individual social opportunities and constraints are transformed at this level to the structural organization—the pattern of social relationships that provides the opportunities and resources, and sets the rules—of the political economy. This position is not premised on the assumption that the whole is the sum of its parts, or on the assumption of the asymmetrical influence these larger macro forces have on social action, but rather on a dynamic approach similar to Anthony Gidden's theory of structuration, which recognizes the recursive nature of social action in social institutions.[7] Individual action is influenced and shaped by the larger structures of society, and at the same time the action shapes and transforms the individual's surroundings.

The social environment prompts individuals to act in certain ways. Through their actions, individuals modify and transform the environment, which in turn will reinforce or change their way of thinking and behavior, and others' as well. To take a simple example of corruption in China, a respondent told the story of her cousin, an assistant manager, who arrived in Beijing with thirty thousand yuan to get an export permit for a product manufactured by his factory. Once in the city, he befriended and showered gifts on the receptionist to get information on the operation of the department and the personality of its chief, and gradually worked his way into the department to know the top administrator. In a month, he left the capital with the permit. This assistant manager knew his action was ethically questionable, but he did it to accomplish his assignment. He had the resources to execute his plan. His factory had given him the money knowing he might need it, and in a way, "legitimized" his action. He succeeded; his action confirmed his own, his superiors', and his friends' perception that this was the way "to get things done." It also reinforced the expectations of the gift recipients that receiving bribes was integral to performing their duties. While the assistant manager's action was prompted by his perception that the government was corrupt, his action added another occurrence to the prevalence of corruption, and encouraged others to do likewise.

The answer to the different propensities of officials for corruption in the two periods is to be found in each period's ideology and structural organization. On the one hand, the moral culture of Chinese society, which has been mostly ignored except in the anthropological analysis on bribery and gift giving, sets both the behavioral guidelines for members of the society and the limits of acceptable behavior. The structural organization, or patterns of relationship governing the positions of the administrators, on the other hand, makes goods available and provides the opportunities for self-enrichment at the same time as it puts constraints on their actions through its rules and supervisory structures. Together, these two aspects of the social environment affect the administrators' propensities to misuse the power vested in their offices, and shape the incidence and nature of corruption in the different periods.

Weakening of Political and Moral Restraints

While China in both the classical socialist and the reform socialist periods can be considered a socialist society the ideologies of the two periods were not alike. Raising production was a primary concern in both eras, but the emphases and methods used to accomplish this goal were different. These differences made for the divergent moral cultures.

In the classical socialist period, raising production was tempered by the effort to restrain materialistic tendencies and a concern for the equal distribution of wealth. The citizenry was constantly reminded that good members of the Communist society should live simply and be ready to sacrifice their individual interests for the collective well-being. This was one reason why the Chinese leaders allowed improvements in the standard of living to fall behind production increases; they wanted to raise output but did not wish the population to be carried away with the pursuit of material comforts.

If ordinary citizens were expected to be so disciplined and altruistic, even more was expected from state officials. Like their traditional Chinese counterparts, Communist managers and officials were required to be models of virtue. The 1957 State Council administrative guidelines encouraged innovativeness, perspicacity, high moral standing, as well as performance from its employees. They were to be frugal and disciplined. Since most high level administrators were trusted party members, they were also subject to the party's behavioral guidelines. The party had similar expectations. Party members were to uphold Communist political ideology and morality, and put the public good and collective interests above family and individual concerns. They were to have "revolutionary courage" and self-respect, and be sincere, frank, and outgoing. This litany of the qualities listed in Liu Shaoqi's "How to Be a Good Communist" was not unlike the Confucian virtues, whereby a *junzi*, or gentleman, had to be self-disciplined, cultivate a high moral standing, and put the interests of the empire before his own. These strict behavioral guidelines suppressed all personal interests and considerations. Failure to live up to these standards would not always constitute corruption, but these yardsticks served to indicate degrees of deviation.

The subculture among officials was reinforced by the larger societal culture. This correspondence between the state and party ideological systems generated an ethos of discipline, asceticism, puritanism, and altruism, which some former state employees had remembered and spoken so proudly of. These orientations discouraged the pursuit of material and personal goals—important motivations for corruption—and set up barriers for those who might want to break administrative or legal regulations. The introduction and consolidation of this ethos among officials in the early fifties were accompanied by a decline in corruption.

This prevailing ethos, of course, did not completely eliminate the problem. As we saw earlier, the family, the rules of reciprocity, the obeisance to one's superiors, and other traditional beliefs and customs encouraged nepotism, bribery, questionable forms of gift giving, and other forms of official abuse of power. The emphasis on commitment to the collective and the multiple layers of collectivities encouraged members to work for their immediate collective or work organizations to make organizational corruption more common in socialist societies than in capitalist ones.

The 1982 work regulations put similar demands on the members of the state bureaucracy. Aside from supporting the party and studying Mao's writings, state employees were to be law abiding, disciplined, humble, civil and polite, cautious, and truthful. They were to lead a simple life; conform to society's mores, be altruistic; and put the interests of the party, the country, and the people ahead of everything else. Government officials were not only to avoid corruption (*tanwu*) and inappropriate behavior (*bu zheng zhi feng*), but to fight them as well. This last exhortation reflects the intrusive and controlling character of Chinese politics; the officials not only had to live up to high standards themselves but also had to ensure that others did the same.

The guidelines, however, lost much of their effectiveness in the changing culture of the seventies and eighties. The reasons were complex and had to be found outside the organization even though their effects ultimately transformed the organizational culture. In the classical socialist period, the subculture of the officials was supported by a similar orientation in the larger society. When the two cultures overlapped, it was easy for the majority of state employees to live according to these standards. Their dedication was buoyed by the optimism of working with a new government and for a renascent nation. Over time, this enthusiasm and novelty wore off; the Chinese government agencies were faced with the inertia and lack of motivation and commitment normal to established bureaucracies.

To some extent, these problems were aggravated by the succession of political campaigns which further undermined faith and commitment to the government. Contemporaneous with the radical economic changes of the Great Leap Forward was the Anti-Rightist Campaign (1957). This was followed by the Socialist Education Movement (1960–1962); the Cultural Revolution (1966–1976); the Criticize Lin Biao, Criticize Confucius Movement (1972); as well as numerous smaller-scale and less dramatic political movements such as the Campaign Against Bourgeois Liberalism (1980–1982), the Anti-Spiritual Pollution Campaign (1983–1984), the Anti-Bourgeois Liberalism Campaign (1987), and the Anti-Peaceful Evolution Campaign (1989).[8] Behind each political campaign with its ideological rhetoric were intense power struggles among the central leaders. Prior to 1966, these struggles were always kept from public view, and the launching of each campaign reaffirmed the triumph and domination of a particular faction. All this changed with the Cultural Revolution. In an attempt to undermine their oppositions, competing factions released or allowed the release of damaging information on their enemies and on their enemies' supporters at the lower levels of government. In traditional Chinese political culture, leaders were often deified and worshipped. Now, these revelations exposed central and local officials as human and vulnerable. During the Cultural Revolution, Liu Shaoqi, the premier and Mao Zedong's presumed successor, together with other leaders, was criticized and vilified. Soon, Lin Biao and the Gang of Four, once Mao Zedong's faithful followers, were held responsible for the chaos of the past decade. After the Cultural Revolution, even Mao's performance was reviewed and found only "70 percent good."

These campaigns, especially the Cultural Revolution, undermined the prestige of the government and the party and the trust state employees had for their leaders at every level. Officials were confused and afraid; administrative staff members were embroiled, if not implicated, in every political campaign. In each new campaign, new heroes were made and new culprits were found; sometimes, the same ones were dragged out to be criticized, making them "veteran athletes," or *lao yundong yuan,* a pun on the word *yundong* meaning sports or campaign, depending on the context. The prestige of the party was damaged and people's faith in the government shattered. After the Cultural Revolution, those criticized during the movement were rehabilitated. Between 1983 and 1987, twenty million who had joined the party in the previous decade were reviewed and 1.5 percent were expelled, put on probation, or punished.[9] These "reversals of verdicts" must have generated intense soul-searching and confusion among both the gainers and losers who had acted out of opportunism or conviction. Worse still, administrators became cynical and skeptical. They lost their commitment and enthusiasm and no longer trusted or respected the government. Even some veteran revolutionaries who fought the guerilla wars of the thirties and forties lost faith in the system and encouraged their children to leave the country. Once these feelings set in, the organizational guidelines for official behavior could not carry the weight or provide the restraint they once did.

Distrust in government was exacerbated by new economic policies that ran counter to some basic Communist ideals and administrative and party guidelines. In the past, there had been a lack of consistency in the economic sphere. In the early fifties, private property was almost wiped out and private markets prohibited. In the early sixties, small private plots and rural markets were allowed, then these efforts at privatization were criticized during the Cultural Revolution. But these changes could not compare with those that took place in the late seventies and eighties. Raising production remained the ultimate goal but it was to be accomplished by the material incentive of having the fruits of labor go to the individual—a complete turnaround from the anti-materialist, egalitarian, and collective orientations of the earlier period and the existing guidelines for official behavior.

The economic policies of the eighties, prompted by pragmatic considerations, violated basic tenets and challenged the fundamentals of Communist ideology. Private property and the accumulation of private wealth were once anathema to communism, which looked to the utopia of collective ownership. The agricultural land lease system, especially when it could be inherited, was strongly reminiscent of private ownership. Owners employing workers and pocketing the profit fitted the socialist definition of exploitation. Accenting profit as the motive and assessment criterion of performance ran counter to the socialist emphasis on collective well-being; allowing the more favorably endowed to move ahead contravened egalitarian principles and widened the income gap, which the previous leaders had striven so hard to close; and dismantling the communes meant abandoning the social welfare responsibilities, which the government once took pride in. Most ideological systems are not completely consistent, but few were so blatantly contradictory as Chinese communism had become in this period.

Despite these departures, the central political leaders still advertised themselves as socialist, and the government and the party as Communist. It was not until the Fourteenth Party Congress in 1992 that the central leaders modified their characterization of the economy by introducing the word "market" and making the Chinese economy a "socialist market economy."[10] The reason might have been political. The party and the leaders justified monopoly of political control by the fact that they stood as the vanguard of the proletariat. Throughout the eighties, they persisted with the traditional Maoist rhetoric and reiterated their adherence to the four basic principles—the socialist road, the proletariat dictatorship, the Communist Party, and Marxist-Leninism and Mao Zedong Thought —while simultaneously introducing measures to dismantle Maoist socialist structures. The intellectual debates of the late seventies and early eighties in the officially controlled newspapers, regarding what constituted profit, exploitation, and equality in socialist societies and the efforts to redefine these terms, perhaps reflected official attempts to reconcile these contradictions at the philosophical level and to introduce some coherence to the dissonance generated among intellectuals.[11]

The new economic policies ran counter to what a whole generation was brought up to believe was right, and the administrative personnel had been carefully screened to include those most committed to these ideals. Many administrators were not convinced by the central leaders' attempts to reconcile the gap between the messages and social reality. Instead, many viewed the efforts of the central leaders as double-talking and double-dealing; and the discrepancy between the leaders' messages and reality as evidence of their hypocrisy. While the legal and administrative guidelines remained consistent in the two eras; the ethos in society did not. The philosophical, if not ideological, inconsistency of the eighties had bred skepticism among the officials, making it easy for them to ignore legal and administrative rules and regulations. By the late eighties, moral restraints were a thing of the past.

Growing Materialism in the Moral Culture

The void in moral authority was filled not only with a revival of religious activities but with a growing materialism and hedonism. Officially, it was now acceptable to make profits and enjoy material comforts. People could take pride in prospering and getting ahead of others. The media in the early eighties carried reports of the "ten thousand yuan households," where peasants became rich working in sideline industries and on land leased from the state; in the late eighties, the stories dealt with successful entrepreneurs who profited from their industrial investments. In a tightly controlled society like China, with a population schooled to follow government directives unquestioningly, it was easy for any new policy to become a fad that overshadowed all other concerns—some citizens compared their behavior to that of a swarm of bees, or *yi wo feng,* with everyone moving in the same direction. The glorification of the successful by the media encouraged the search for material wealth and the better life until it became a national preoccupation. Those who attained wealth displayed it in conspicuous consumption, those who did not have it tried their best to attain it. However, legitimizing material comforts and incentives, especially at a time of weakening norms, provided a motivation for corruption and going after larger amounts because corruption was, after all, primarily a crime against property.

With the replacement of sacrifice and altruism as the social ideal by material wealth, administrative cadres lost much of the social status they had derived from their positions. In the past, their superiority had rested on their education, their political conformity, and the power of their office. Now the values attached to education, political conformity, and clout were supplanted by material wealth, which was not necessarily acquired through education or by obeying official norms. Money could buy anything. It should not be surprising that many state employees as corporate citizens of the new society, who in the past had proven most receptive to official ideology, would embrace the new value of materialism with equal ease and alacrity. They were, after all, generally the most ambitious and the most adaptive of their cohort. They felt they had lost ground in improving their financial circumstances when compared to the other sectors of society, and the new individualistic ethos suggested that it was up to them to rectify the situation even by breaking rules.[12] One sympathetic former administrator defended such colleagues, saying that they had to survive (*shenghuo*). I am not sure if survival was at stake, but a way of life was. If they wanted to maintain their once superior lifestyle, they had to look for resources outside their regular income, and many were successful in their attempts to get recompensation. The growing corruption and the success with which dishonest cadres enriched themselves seemed to be an affirmation of the power of state officials, despite the changing basis of power in the eighties.

What seems to be at issue is the social or material position of state officials relative to other sectors of society. The officials lost out in the reform socialist period. Private entrepreneurs flaunted their wealth in ways that sometimes even state officials could not match. Furthermore, it was no longer enough to enjoy luxuries on the job when there was the option and possibility of owning property outright. Some compensated for their lost advantage through malfeasance which by now included not just getting entertainment at public expense, but embezzlement, bribery, and more clearcut forms of corruption to augment their personal wealth and satisfy their material needs. There might be some truth in the suggestion that raising the salary of these employees might counteract the attractiveness of corruption and raise the stakes if detected.[13] But few governments could match the amount successful business persons could earn in a land of opportunity as China was in the eighties. The question would be to find the suitable or satisfactory level of income for this group, which again is deeply embedded in the values of the society, and which the government could afford.

The new relaxed economic policies were intended to encourage individual and organizational initiatives, to raise production, and to make profit, which would ultimately be reinvested in production. However, businesses reinvest only if they have faith in the status quo; in the early eighties, they did not. Despite government reasssurances of its long-term commitment to such policies, many remembered the previous sharp turns in the official line and remained distrustful. Instead of reinvesting surplus funds in production or long-term projects, individuals and state and collective enterprises hid their surplus from the center, invested the money in the construction of clubhouses and residences, or divided their profit among their members as bonuses or other fringe benefits. Many spent the money they received on material enjoyment. The search for immediate gratification and the display of newly acquired wealth fanned further conspicuous consumption and provided even stronger motivation to pursue material wealth. The cases of corruption increased, but the monetary value involved in these cases also jumped.

Confusion about official ideology and distrust of the government encouraged people to seek security in the particularistic culture they once knew. In the classical socialist period, the government encouraged reliance on the state and not the family; but it had never succeeded in weaning the population completely from their personal ties. With their faith in the state shaken and the new emphasis on individual effort, people turned once more to the security of family and friends. Furthermore, the limited forms of private ownership now sanctioned by the state often relied on the pooled efforts of family members, thus legitimizing dependence on the private realm of family in economic endeavors. Consequently, personal connections figured more prominently in the culture of the eighties than in the classical socialist period; the importance attached to these ties, as we have seen in chapter 4, provided the motivation for corruption. Moreover, it was no longer important to become rich just for themselves, but state employees felt a responsibility to do the same for their families and friends. These considerations led to the justification of corruption and the proliferation of nepotism, which had never been completely rooted out in any case, even in the classical socialist period.

As personal ties and relationships gained new importance, so did gift giving—the traditional form of expressions of intimacy, trust, respect, and obligations.[14] This ritual, formerly accepted in the traditional particularistic society, was condemned in the socialist one and not without reason. The Chinese socialist culture, like capitalist cultures, subscribed to universalistic and not particularistic rules. In its emphasis on the collective at the expense of the private realm, the application of universalistic criteria and not personalized standards was all the more vigorous. In the eighties, the practice of gift giving gained new popularity, but the reemergence of past practices was never a simple replay of the past. Now, the essence of gift giving had been transformed from an act to seal personal social relationships to become something more instrumental and impersonal. It was sometimes a simple market transaction used to mask bribery and corruption.

Just as the commitment to collective interest under classical socialism had encouraged false reporting and organizational corruption, the new materialistic political culture and the weakening moral restraints under reform socialism had inadvertently provided new pressures and incentives for more varied kinds of corruption. The acquisition of money and other material comforts became important goals in these transactions. The new emphasis on individualism and individual efforts encouraged state employees to benefit themselves and their families as well as their organizations. The growing attachment to family and friends now sanctioned in the search for new norms of behavior and security only increased nepotism and provided further justification for breaking rules to obtain ever higher returns.

New Opportunities in the Political Economic Structures

Political economic structures, like their cultural counterparts, offer both incentives and restraints to corruption. In chapter 3, I discussed in some detail how the centralization of power and the almost complete dependence of officials on higher authorities under socialism put pressure on units to file false reports and opened up opportunities for the abuse of state resources. Here, I shall focus on how the new organizational arrangements introduced under reform socialism encouraged and produced varied forms of corruption.

Although the Chinese official channels and some social scientists have characterized organizational changes under reform socialism as decentralization, labeling these changes as such can be misleading. In the early eighties, the central government did not relinquish its decision-making power in the planning of the economy, it only gave more power to the local organizations. Sharing power is not a zero-sum game where one player's gain is always at the expense of another; new powers can be created and delegated. In China, economic units still had to fulfill performance quotas and had their supplies guaranteed by the state, but they could use any resources saved during production or materials obtained from the free market in outside-plan production and retain the profits from this source after remitting a portion as tax. Otherwise, there was no change in the authority structure at any level, and decentralization in China was not necessarily associated with democratization or greater participation in decision making, as we understand it in the West.

On the contrary, the authority of the unit heads within the organizations became stronger as a result of these changes in "decentralization." One man's management was still enforced and the unit chief controlled production and all aspects of the employees' lives. Even in the villages where the communes were dismantled, the separation of economic and political power was more academic than real.[15] Discharged political leaders often became managers of the newly created and highly profitable rural enterprises. Now that grass-roots units had decision-making power in the use of their local resources, in outside-plan production, and in the control of its outside-plan profits, unit heads acquired new powers in running their organizations. These new arrangements in a growing economy also meant more profit for the local unit, which in effect meant more resources under the administrators' jurisdiction. With more materials to give out, these unit heads had more they could give to their employees, and the latter became more beholden to them.

The greater power given to unit heads and to state administrators in general offered them more opportunities for corruption. Perpetrators of corruption were after all not the romantic rebels resisting the system; they were mostly the privileged who were in a position to take advantage of the weaknesses in the system—this is precisely why rules on corruption in China were aimed at administrators who had access to all kinds of goods and therefore were more likely to indulge in corruption than others. Dishonest administrators used the opportunities available to them on the job to benefit themselves—purchasing agents demanded commissions from their suppliers, sales agents wanted higher prices for goods in demand and payments on the side, engineers wanted bribes for delivering blueprints or getting work done on time, tax agents would lower the taxes of those who humored them, and inspectors and licensing agents had to be paid if their authorization was required.[16]

The access to greater material wealth in a climate of growing attachment to material well-being and weakening moral restraints contributed not only to the rising incidence of corruption but also to the increased value of the property involved. There is the case of Zhang Shiyan, the lowly administrative cadre who embezzled eleven thousand yuan between 1971 and 1975. With the introduction of fiscal reforms, which made more money available at the lower level, he got away with even more: 226,762 yuan and meal tickets worth 4,361 *jin* of grain between 1976 and 1979—twice as much as during the earlier period and without a change in his position.[17] The greater sums embezzled or spent on eating and drinking and on building luxurious offices, clubhouses, and residences during this period too can be attributed in part to the accessibility of growing wealth at these levels.

Corruption is a business transaction or an exploitative situation in which the party with more leverage or greater clout gets the better deal—state officials usually receive the benefits and their clients, the "victims," pay. This period witnessed an increase in the number of private houses and other amenities, but these provisions were available only to those who could afford them, such as the nouveau riche or those with overseas connections. Most of the labor force still looked to their work units to satisfy their needs. The increased local resources augmented the administrative cadres' abilities to provide for such needs and thereby strengthened their hold over unit members as well as the former's ability to impose legal or illegal demands on the workers. In addition, their power to deliver made them more likely targets of bribery. The broad powers of the administrative leaders in operation and in personnel made them susceptible to corruption in the new era.

With the growing economy and more wealth at the grass roots, their clients were more willing and had more money with which to grease palms than in the classical era. The growing affluence to some extent explains the increased number and rising monetary value in corruption cases.

The greater dependence on the work unit also strengthened the members' attachment to these smaller collectives vis-à-vis the larger one of the society and increased the propensity for organizational crimes. In the past, a "perverted" sense of collective interest, at least in the eyes of the center, had prompted production units to hide resources from above to enhance their overall performance. They continued to do so, only now it was to provide the wherewithal to engage in private production to improve the lot of their workers. The occasional reports of managers being attacked or killed by workers for failing to meet the latters' demands were enough motivation for all administrators to expend their energies in this direction. Administrators sometimes transferred resources allocated to produce state goods to private production activities to the extent that factories failing to meet the state quota might have "excess" goods for sale in the market. Furthermore, with private market prices much higher than negotiated or state prices, factories or companies made more profit selling their goods in this arena than to the state, and there was no way the government could distinguish within-quota from above-quota products so as to police the circulation of these goods.

Enterprises engaged in private production activities were to pay a 55 percent profit tax that was adjustable according to the specific situation of the firm.[18] With their supplies for private production coming from questionable sources, such as materials which should have been used to manufacture state goods, managers were disinclined to report these outputs or their profits. Moreover, this form of taxation was a novel practice among state enterprises; many individuals and units regarded this as a burden and an unfair state procurement. Consequently, many units underreported their profits and tax evasion was widespread. In the rural areas, tax collectors were sometimes attacked and thrown off the property. The more civil bribed the tax assessors instead. Since these government officials could reduce taxes for new enterprises or businesses that had attracted foreign investments, work units paid them to misuse their discretionary power.

Enterprises not only sold state goods in the market to earn extra profit, but more often their activities bordered on speculation. This form of corruption was made possible by the institution of dual ownership and free markets. As in the early fifties, the coexistence of private and state companies facilitated questionable and quasi-legal transactions; dishonest state officials collaborated with private companies to make personal profits. Instead of selling their products directly to another state company that needed the goods, sometimes state firms sold the goods to private firms, which in turn raised the price before selling the goods to another state company. The resulting profit was split among the participants. This practice stopped when the Chinese government took over the distribution of goods, but it reemerged in the eighties when the state relinquished some of these powers. Speculation became even more attractive with the advent of a multiple pricing system. In a market with no price controls, prices find their equilibrium and fluctuate with supply and demand. In the heated economy and feverish construction activities of reform socialism, the demand for steel, cement, fertilizers, and other materials needed in capital construction drove up prices, making them much higher than those paid by the state. Some of this increase, however, was artificial, driven by speculative activities that led to an ever upward spiral. State companies sold their supplies of low-cost and subsidized state goods to private or other state companies, which in turn sold them again. With each transaction, a profit was made and prices rose sometimes five or six times without the goods ever leaving the warehouse. The money, of course, might go to the work unit or the individual. These illicit transactions were dubbed *guandao* (speculation by officials) because only administrators with access to materials could engage in these activities.

In addition to the demand for capital goods, there was great demand for consumer goods. The increase in money available at the grass roots created greater buying power, which, together with the acceptance of limited forms of private property and of conspicuous consumption, generated demand for consumer items. Those who could afford to bought houses; most wanted televisions, stereos, refrigerators, motor bicycles, and other brand-name products. Work organizations wanted motor vehicles, furniture, and other luxury items. Consumer demand and the resulting shortage of supplies provided the opportunity not only for bribery and speculation but also for consumer fraud and smuggling. In the rich rural areas, the pressure for land to build new houses had dishonest officials defying state regulations and turning agricultural land into lots for residences for themselves and for their clients, and in later years, leasing them to developers for a fee.[19] I have discussed earlier how state or collective factories manufactured ersatz goods, how department stores adulterated their goods or imposed slow-sale items on their clients, and how different branches of the government collaborated in smuggling. Enterprises could not have acted in these ways with impunity if demand had not exceeded supply or if buyers were unwilling or unable to pay.

In the eighties, the opportunities for corruption grew with the increased power delegated to state employees, and the economic arrangements offered numerous and novel opportunities for corruption. Dishonest state employees capitalized on their own capabilities and the demands of the situation in picking the easiest ways to benefit themselves. The earlier period offered corruption opportunities characteristic of a socialist system, but a system straddling socialism and capitalism carried opportunities found in both systems and also generated new contradictions and loopholes that clever but dishonest civil servants could use. Corrupt practices characteristic of socialism such as false reporting, hoarding, and wastefulness proliferated in this situation of uncertainty, rapid changes, and constant flux; the hybrid planned economy with its dual markets, private/state companies, and multi-pricing system provided access to new opportunities. The free market in the Chinese planned economy allowed producers to use supplies of raw materials hidden from the state for private production. The multiple pricing system let them sell subsidized state goods in the open market at a great profit, and the private companies offered a cover for illegal activities and a channel for hiding illicit gains. China in the eighties was a land of opportunity for the well-positioned but dishonest administrator who wanted to become rich, and the opportunities offered shaped the kinds of corruption that occurred.

Lack of Structural Controls

In a highly centralized system such as China's, structural constraints operated more effectively within organizations than between organizations in different echelons. Within the organization, those at the top wielded enormous power. Administrators were responsible only to their superiors and never accountable to their inferiors. Their power came from the authority necessary to allow them to carry out the work assigned to their positions. It also came from their control of the resources essential to the well-being of their staffs. This authority structure, plus the physical arrangement of the work units, where workplace and residence were often located in one compound or in close proximity with each other, meant that the workers' every public and private activity was closely watched by both their superiors and fellow workers. From their defensive and dependent position, subordinates seldom questioned the superiors' authority or the appropriateness of organizational rules.

Leaders of Chinese organizations had an additional prerogative rarely enjoyed by their counterparts in the West. Transgressions of administrative rules and sometimes even laws were handled internally by the work organization; administrators would refer legal cases to the courts only if they believed that the accused were guilty of serious offenses. Even then they would be reluctant to do so because these cases would reflect badly on the organization and might even be interpreted as the lack of effective leadership and supervision on their part. Inside the work unit, the party's disciplinary committee and the administration's supervisory committee oversaw rule transgressions among the employees. Like the criminal justice system, the administration's supervisory committee did not function between 1957 and 1979, and the party disciplinary committees took over such duties in both divisions. They, too, were abolished between 1968 and 1979, but the party secretaries never abandoned their judicial and policing functions.

When rules were broken, the party secretary qua administrator was prosecutor, investigator, judge, and executor of justice all rolled into one. The accused could respond to the charges and appeal, but the party's judgment was almost always final. The party could warn the guilty or, in severe cases, dismiss them from their jobs or from the party itself. In Chinese society, where the work organization and the party played such an important role in a person's life, punishment by dismissal was disaster enough. However, those found guilty of political crimes by the work organization could be incarcerated in labor camps without ever appearing in court. This combination of the judicial roles and the administrators' discretionary power in meting out rewards and punishments made their authority unassailable within the organization.

Within an organization, institutionalized means to police the behavior of the workers at each level were in place, but there was no equivalent to police the top administrators at each of these levels or subunits. This was the reason why Chinese administrators actually involved in administration were seen as more prone to abuse of power and other forms of corruption than administrators involved in professional work, such as purchasing, accounting, or engineering. The latters' power was more restricted and their operations were often supervised by these administrative personnel. Not only did these administrative administrators control the resources within the unit, they were the final arbitrator of "justice" accountable to no one at that level and only to the superior outside that unit.

The absence of institutions to monitor the performance of the top administrator within an organization was one reason why wining and dining investigation teams and false reporting to curry superiors' favor were common in China. Organizations that were higher in the hierarchy had limited means to validate the claims or the authenticity of the reports from their subordinate units. Instead, the Communist government relied heavily on careful screening in the selection of candidates for administrative positions. Ideological education started early in school, and the behavior of students was closely watched both inside and outside the classroom. Organizations like the Young Pioneers and the Young Communist League offered further training grounds for those with leadership potential. The development of each and every student was carefully recorded in individual dossiers. Only those with impeccable political records indicating willingness to conform to and enthusiasm for the Communist ideals could be considered eligible for higher education, an administrative job, or promotion to higher ranks. Throughout the individual's working life, political education continued in the form of frequent ideological campaigns; the broad dissemination and repetition of political messages in the media; and regular meetings in the work units where participants discussed central directives, expressed their commitment to the party, and exposed their innermost thoughts toward the government and its policies.

The smooth functioning of this hierarchical system rested on the commitment of those at the top and their willingness to abide by and enforce the rules. It also depended on a vestige of traditional Chinese culture. At the risk of repetition, one has to remember that officials were considered "parents" of the people, who looked after their wards' interests. It was a personalistic system in which regulations were seldom consulted and leaders had great discretion. For this reason, until the 1979 rules, regulations governing corruption were phrased in broad amorphous terms, encapsulating the spirit and morality of the times rather than giving clearcut guidelines or definitions of behavior. The rulers, as exemplars of virtue, were to be carefully observed as models by their subordinates. Effective governance rested on the moral authority of the rulers, not on physical force. When rulers broke the rules and wandered from the·moral standards of the society, they lost their legitimacy and their power. Those below would ignore their rules or directives, or, worse still, in the case of corruption, the subordinates would follow the leaders' examples, though they might be too timid to expose their superiors. This was what the Chinese call *shang xing xia xiao*—when actions (now usually bad) of those at the top are imitated by those below.

This rule by example can explain, besides the careful selection process, the relative lack of written regulations and corruption among the administrative ranks in the classical socialist period. In the fifties, the population saw their central leaders as dedicated and the civil service as committed—people who abided by the organizational and legal rules. Those below followed suit. Officials still might enjoy perks denied the population, but because of the high status given to Chinese officials, the people could accept a certain degree of such transgressions or gray corruption as rites befitting their official ranks. In the period of reform socialism, central leaders were exposed as participants in corruption. For example, the 1985 central directive explicitly forbade children of cadres to engage in business, but the 1989 high-profile case concerning Kang Hua Development Corporation and four other companies only confirmed what the population knew all along—children of politburo members were involved in business, tax evasion, and speculation.[20] Chinese citizens resented the way top leaders introduced and imposed laws only to break them. If the top leaders and their children could do it, so could they.

Consequently, despite the government's attempt to institutionalize legal reforms in the eighties, this method of structuring constraints was never effective. The situation was further complicated by the fact that the government failed to anticipate the rapid and dramatic changes brought on by the new economic policies.

The 1979 criminal code was simplistic and flawed with loopholes that state officials easily took advantage of. Anything not specifically proscribed in the legal documents was permissible. Even when these opportunities were plugged, many who had benefited from these activities found it hard to quit and simply ignored the laws. In a tradition where the leaders' examples set limits of appropriate behavior, the proliferation of laws and regulations alone could not stop the corrupt behavior of the civil service. Clearly, administrators who themselves were involved in corruption would be reluctant to enforce the regulations or pursue those who transgressed them.

Outside monitoring agencies were equally ineffective. Each economic unit was usually nested in a powerful ministry or government department that jealously guarded its own jurisdiction and resented outside interference. The criminal justice system resuscitated in 1979 was young and weak in comparison to these powerful economic units. The courts operated at the will of the powerful government departments as they chose the cases to be relegated to the criminal justice system; neither would the courts have much chance of success should they pursue cases without the cooperation of these units. Many of the leaders in the criminal justice system were recruited from the People's Liberation Army with little legal training and chosen probably for their loyalty to the Communist Party rather than for their expertise. They did not have trained legal staff nor did they have strong influence in the localities, especially when compared with the leaders of these powerful economic units and their well-established networks.

Neither did the other newly created monitoring agencies have much success. In 1983 the government created an auditing department and in the late eighties a public relations branch to investigate citizens' complaints. Again, these departments were understaffed and vested with few powers. These nascent organizations were no match for the established government departments and enterprises in their jostling for power, and were often bullied by their more powerful rivals into acquiescence. Therefore, with the breakdown of informal self-imposed moral and social constraints and the absence of effective structural controls, there were few safeguards or deterrents to prevent dishonest officials from capitalizing on the increasing opportunities for corruption.

Growing Momentum of Corruption

In the jargon of popular criminology, the criminal needs a motive and an opportunity. But motives and opportunities are shorthand labels for complex congeries of cultural and social factors that can influence individuals to pursue certain behavior patterns. I have analyzed the four major influences at work in Chinese society: the cultural motivators and constraints, and the structure of opportunities and constraints. The sources of these changes originated from outside the work units but they changed the work environment in which these administrators exercised their power. Changes of the eighties undermined their commitment to the organization rules, increased the attractiveness of material gains, magnified their prerogatives, but without adding effective constraints to corruption. Each of these aspects had its own complex internal structures that affected corruption, and together their imprints shaped the pattern of corruption and its evolution in China between 1949 and 1989, propelling it to move in certain directions and take certain forms.

In the classical socialist period, the acquisition of material wealth was considered wrong. The poor economic conditions provided few accessible targets for corruption; the ownership structure, together with the puritanical social climate, put strong restraints on anyone who might consider breaking legal or administrative rules. Instead, state employees were encouraged to work for their collectives, and the opportunities to sacrifice themselves for the larger good were plentiful. Consequently, illegitimate activities in this period fell mainly into the gray area of corruption, with administrators enjoying perks on the job or, more frequently, hiding resources from the center or doctoring official reports to benefit the organization.

In the reform socialist period, the puritanical and ascetic culture was replaced by an individualistic and materialistic one that provided incentives for becoming rich. A law-abiding state administrator on a relatively fixed income had little chance of becoming the head of a "ten thousand yuan household." Although the legitimate means for making their fortunes were closed, their positions as administrators generally gave them access to money and material goods. In a climate of declining respect for the central government, where legal institutional controls were ineffective, both moral and structural restraints on these state employees were weak. Consequently, the incidence of corruption and the value of the property involved rose and the forms of corruption proliferated.

In China, where leaders were vested with unlimited power and divided on their vision of the future society, a change in the leaders could bring about dramatic transformation in social conditions and attitudes. Such was the case in 1976. The new set of leaders brought dramatic changes to the country. Once the effects of these large changes registered on individuals, they created a chain reaction. A person's way of thinking and behaving is shaped by the larger social climate, and such actions in turn can reinforce, modify, or change the environment. If a person feels satisfied with or is rewarded for a particular action, the tendency to continue the behavior is likely to be reinforced. If the activity is punished or found to be distasteful, it is likely to be discontinued. These processes of reproduction contributed to the growing momentum, though in different directions, in the evolution of corruption in China during the two eras.

Corruption was not unusual in the beginning of the classical socialist period, but the Communist government took summary measures and severely punished the guilty. The harsh punishments struck fear among employees. More importantly, the political leaders projected the image of honesty, diligence, dedication and self-sacrifice. Their persistent ideological campaigns instilled pride in the civil service for ascetism, discipline, altruism, and success in overcoming the temptation of breaking the organizational and legal rules. The government and society rewarded state employees not with material goods but with honor, public recognition, and promotion, which were equally satisfying and further weaned them from materialistic attachments. Conformity bred conformity. In such a social climate, individuals would find it easier to follow than to break state regulations and laws or to indulge in questionable behavior to benefit themselves materially at the risk of being punished by their superiors or ostracized by their peers.

In the eighties, circumstances changed, which in turn modified the behavior of Chinese officials. The materialistic orientation of the official media and of society at large overshadowed the ascetic code of the administrative regulations, the new economic structure offered numerous opportunities for enrichment. Some administrators, succumbing to materialism, chose the easiest and most profitable but questionable way to become rich. Sometimes, they achieved this by breaking administrative rules. In doing so, and if they were not caught, they achieved the socially acceptable goal of making their own lives more comfortable as well as, sometimes, those of their families, friends, and staffs. Thus, they gained the positive reinforcement of admiration and envy of those around them. With success, their chances of repeating such actions increased and others followed.

Such exploits were facilitated by practices in the traditional culture, where gift giving and cultivating personal relationships were the norms. In the uncertainties of the new society, traditional practices, such as the exchange of gifts on festive occasions, gained greater popularity. These rituals, traditionally used to seal bonds among members of the family and also with one's superiors, presented excellent opportunities or subterfuges for cadres to receive bribes. In addition, the hierarchical orientation in traditional Confucian teachings, together with structured dependence of the staffs on the organization under socialism, cemented the superior position of these administrators. Their hold in the industrial work units and in the rural areas remained, but their influences were exercised through different channels. Rural cadres, for example, no longer directly assigned peasants production responsibilities; however, the links these cadres once established during their term of office were useful in helping peasants secure bank loans and supplies, or in extricating them from difficult situations. This real and learned dependence on their superiors arising from the socialist organizational structures and from tradition silenced the population, making them reluctant to report any irregularities.

Those who live in glass houses do not throw stones. The administrators' illegitimate involvements discouraged them from reporting any transgressions of regulations by colleagues or from punishing their subordinates for doing likewise. To do so would only invite accusations and exposure of their own misconduct from others, and the transgressors were bound by a code of silence. Thus, a safe climate for corruption evolved, and, in the end, it became so common that the probability of success outweighed the chances of being caught.

Corrupt practices became such a normal part of existence that they no longer evoked moral distaste and were accepted as the way to do business. Dishonest officials used their power to acquire what they could from public and private sources. Those needing anything from officials would bring a gift with them without asking. Those who adhered to the norm of abstaining from dishonest actions found themselves, at the very least, materially disadvantaged compared with their peers, and sometimes considered stupid or even ostracized by their colleagues. The proliferation of corruption created a situation that only further reinforced and encouraged such activities. In this way, corruption evolved, developed, and became embedded in Chinese governmental structures and in the society at large.

Notes

1. Nathaniel H. Leff, "Economic Development through Bureaucratic Corruption," *American Behavioral Scientist* 8, no. 3 (November 1964): 8–14.

2. Jean C. Oi, *State and Peasant in Contemporary China: The Political Economy of Village Government* (Berkeley: University of California Press, 1989).

3. Peter Nan-shong Lee, "Bureaucratic Corruption During the Deng Xiaoping Era," *Corruption and Reform* 5 (1990): 29–47.

4. Mayfair Mei-hui Yang, "The Gift Economy and State Power in China," *Comparative Studies in Society and History* 31, no. 1 (January 1989): 25–54.

5. Ronald Wraith and Edgar Simpkins, *Corruption in Developing Countries* (New York: Norton, 1963).

6. Liu Cuiping, "On the Identity Between Opposing Bourgeois Liberation and Anti Corruption," *Guangming Ribao,* June 30, 1990, p. 3; He Jiacheng, "Rectification and Economic Reform," *Fazhan yu Gaige* (1989): 18–25; Liu Leizhong and Wang Chende, "Reasons of Growth and Economic Role of Local Governments at Present: An Analysis," *Zhongguo: Fazhan yu Gaige* 1 (1988): 42–48, quoted in Gong Ting, *The Politics of Corruption in Contemporary China* (Westport, Conn.: Praeger, 1994), pp. 21–22

7. Anthony Giddens, *The Constitution of Society: Outline of the Theory of Structuration* (Berkeley: University of California Press, 1984).

8. Charles Cell, *Revolution at Work: Mobilization Campaigns in China* (New York: Academic Press, 1977).

9. Suzanne Ogden, *China's Unresolved Issues: Politics, Development, and Culture* (Englewood Cliffs, N.J.: Prentice Hall, 1989), pp. 126–27.

10. *Renmin Ribao,* October 17, 1992, p.1.

11. Lin Wei and Arnold Chao, *China's Economic Reforms* (Philadelphia: University of Pennsylvania Press, 1982). This is a book written by academics in China and the introduction clearly articulates the importance of measuring policies by results and not by abstract principles.

12. Anita Chan, Richard Madsen, and Jonathan Unger, *Chen Village Under Mao and Deng* (Berkeley: University of California Press, 1992), p. 293, showed how comparison with relatives in Hong Kong could promote crimes.

13. Gary S. Becker and George J. Stigler, "Law Enforcement, Malfeasance, and Compensation of Enforcers," *Journal of Legal Studies* 3, no. 1 (January 1974): 6.

14. *Renmin Ribao,* September 29, 1978, p. 3.

15. Chan, Madsen, and Unger, *Chen Village,* p. 318.

16. Ole Bruun, *Business and Bureaucracy in a Chinese City: An Ethnography of Private Business Households in Contemporary China* (Berkeley: University of California, Institute of East Asian Studies, 1993), chapter 5.

17. *Renmin Ribao,* October 11, 1980, p. 3.

18. Carl Riskin, *China's Political Economy: The Quest for Development Since 1949* (New York: Oxford University Press, 1987), p. 346.

19. Jean Louis Rocca, "Corruption and Its Shadow: An Anthropological View of Corruption in China," *China Quarterly,* no. 130 (June 1992): 402–16.

20. *Renmin Ribao,* August 17, 1989; Louise do Rosario, "Big Four, Less One," *Far Eastern Economic Review,* November 17, 1988, pp. 91–92; Anne F. Thurston, *A Chinese Odyssey: The Life and Times of a Chinese Dissident* (New York: Charles Scribner's Sons, 1991), pp. 401–2.

6

A Look to the Future

Eight years have passed since the citizens of Beijing demonstrated against government corruption on Tian'anmen Square. The anti-corruption campaigns launched in the aftermath of these demonstrations increased the supervision of state employees, and intensified the pressure on officials to follow administrative rules. These measures temporarily reduced corruption. But without any fundamental changes in the cultural climate and opportunity structures, the incidence of corruption and shady financial transactions have surpassed those of the eighties.

At the same time, some forms of corruption popular in the late eighties declined. For example, the elimination of the double pricing system discouraged speculation in many capital goods sectors. Nevertheless, those in charge of these resources are still in a position to make illicit gains because of high demand in a booming economy. Moreover, the decline in speculation has been more than offset by new forms of corruption that accompanied the introduction of stock exchanges, the electronic transfer of money in banking, and the growth of the real estate market. Rules regulating the financial market are few and those in place are often ignored. Insider-trading and other such abuses are rampant, and speculation in stocks and shares involving hundreds of thousands and even millions of yuan has supplanted speculation in material goods. Returns from the stock market have become so attractive that dishonest cadres are willing to take shares instead of cash for bribes. Minor state functionaries without easy access to lucrative schemes embezzle public funds to acquire capital for investment. The electronic transfer of money has made supervision and detection more difficult, thus making it easy for dishonest banking officials to divert money to other purposes. Those successful in the stock market quickly return the money they have peculated and remain undetected; those charged lose their capital and cannot repay. Leasing land belonging to the state in the name of development is popular in the rural areas, and these real estate transactions have left millions in local coffers with few enforceable guidelines on how these funds are to be disbursed. As a consequence, dishonest officials spend money on entertainment and questionable projects as well as divesting considerable sums to their private accounts, leaving communities with only a small fraction of the returns.

Such novel forms of malfeasance contribute to a continued overall climate of corruption these days. Because the atmosphere, attitudes and economic structures of the eighties have remained intact, one should not expect any radical change regarding corruption in China. Nor should one be surprised that the momentum of corruption has increased and intensified.

The conclusions drawn from the analysis of the eighties still apply. Corrupt administrators in the economic sector are not attempting to undermine the system; they are agents entrusted by the system with power but exploiting it for their personal gains. At best, they may be seen as survivors caught up in a chaotic and conflicting set of pressures and demands from the different quarters who seek only to better their lives. At worse, they appear as predators and opportunists taking advantage of their superiors, clients, and subordinates. In any case, their actions are made possible only because they have the powers to do so. Corruption is, after all, using one's institutional office for personal gains. And this is possible because political and economic values and structures facilitate if not encourage such practices.

Chinese and Western Modes of Corruption

In the period 1949–1989 venal economic administrators engaged in fraud (false reporting and doctoring documents), bribery, extortion, theft, embezzlement, speculation, smuggling, and other abuses. The illegitimate activities of these state or collective factory directors, managers of trading companies, department heads as well as technical personnel were not so different from those of their Western counterparts. Although they do not own these businesses, they have certain managerial rights and obligations that are subject to abuse. But corruption, like models of development in China, also has unique Chinese characteristics. Let us review some of the more important similarities and differences between Western and Chinese corruption.

Administrators in the West engage in nepotism, but not with the same frequency or to the same extent as have their Chinese opposites who put primary importance on the family and personal relationships. Western administrators profit from speculative activities, taking advantage of price variations over time or in different localities, but these are accepted practices. The government intervenes only when they try to corner and monopolize markets. For more than thirty years, the Chinese government monopolized the economy. Only in the eighties did Chinese administrators speculate on the gaps between state and market prices, and by the nineties begin to take advantage of the weak stock market regulations to carry out insider trading. Chinese administrators fabricated reports and expended state resources on banquets, buildings, and other practices to obtain "empty" honors, or face, that carried little direct material gain but might prepare the way for future profit. In the more materialistic and affluent West, dishonest administrators would be reluctant to take these risks for such small rewards. They might not be prosecuted but they might lose their employment. Neither would they follow the examples of their Chinese counterparts in the classical socialist period by embezzling or dishonestly using state resources to boost their companies' production; these resources are simply out of their reach. Nor would they illegally stock materials for their companies' future use; this would only tie up their capital. They would more likely use or sell these resources as fast as possible. Powerful companies in the West would bribe legislators for regulations favorable to their operation; Chinese ones would not do that because these decision-makers are too few and inaccessible. Instead they focus on the implementers getting them to bend state rules. Even during reform socialism, when individualism was the prevailing ethos, many Chinese administrators defrauded the state only to divide a substantive share of their illicit gains among the workers. If administrators in the West took similar action, they would more likely keep the gains for themselves.

In general, corrupt executives in the West go for money first, and then non-monetary material resources. But given the shortage of material goods, Chinese administrators had different priorities. In the absence of private ownership in the first thirty years after the Communists came to power, they had few resources apart from those derived from their jobs. Dishonest officials, not unlike their predecessors in the feudal past, bullied their underlings to supply their needs, provide services, or cater to their wishes in ways that would only be possible for people with almost absolute power. With a more vocal clientele, Western administrators in the economic sector would never be able to get away with such bureaucratic misconduct.

Some dishonest Chinese state employees indulged in clearcut cases of corruption, much like those of any society where state officials milk the government and their clients for their own benefit. But much of what was done, especially when the state dominated in the classical socialist period, would fall into a gray area where defining certain actions as corrupt and hence criminal might be debatable. In the West, spending company funds on lavish entertainment may come from budgets set aside for public relations or marketing. Hoarding raw materials, and exaggerating individual accomplishments or inflating a unit's output may be considered bad judgment or improper behavior, but not corruption. Company shareholders might object to "indiscriminate" spending on expensive capital expenditures, but Western governments generally ignore instances of executives' spending company funds on office buildings and other such amenities, and indeed might even praise them for promoting their workers' welfare.

A Political Economic Interpretation

The differences between corrupt practices in China and in the West rest on their distinct political economies. Chinese socialist ideology defined "public" broadly, put great emphasis on collective well-being, and viewed any action promoting "private" interest as selfish and disloyal even when these actions benefit the work units. Furthermore, because of the national need for both resources and development, the leadership took a jaundiced view of anyone who wasted state property or withheld resources for one's work units, and condemned the tradition of putting one's family's interests first. Consequently, any attempt to convert state property into that of the smaller collective, let alone providing for friends or family or taking possession of property for individual use, was considered corrupt, that is, using public office for private gain. In practice, this official understanding of corruption was tempered by the Chinese tradition of the tolerance for officials enjoying special privileges and by the sympathetic understanding extended to those working for family and friends. Still the socialist definition of corruption was much more restrictive and covered a broader array of activities than the Western one in which persons who amass private property and strive for individual success are admired.

No political economic system is free from corruption. Every complex organization has to delegate powers to its agents in the discharge of their duties. Such arrangements thus provide officials the opportunities to abuse their powers if they choose to do so. Nor can a society socialize its members so successfully that every functionary will comply with all organizational rules and follow them at all times. Both socialist and capitalist systems condemn corruption or keep it to acceptable levels that do not compromise performance, but no society has been able to eradicate it. There are always those who find ways to beat or use the system.

Since my focus is on corruption in socialist China, I have not dwelled on its manifestation in a predominantly capitalist society.

Nor do I want to draw from the above observations any conclusion on human nature or even to get into a philosophical discussion on this topic; finding the answer as to why humans indulge in corrupt behavior is the task of philosophers. Instead, I am interested in how culture and social structures affect the exercise of power among officials and which may, in turn, lead to corruption in China.

In the forty years between 1949 and 1989, the incidence, values, and the forms of corruption among Chinese state employees fluctuated in what may be described as an elongated U curve, with the final point higher than the initial one. When these forty years are divided into the two periods of classical and reform socialism, the pre-1976 society had fewer cases of corruption involving less money and fewer people than did the post-1976 society. This study, tracing the changes in the political economy and corruption over a forty-year period, makes no claim to providing a general etiology of corruption in socialist societies, but comparing the two periods can provide a better understanding of how specific features of the Chinese socialist system affected corruption, and may provide us with clues as to its dynamics in other settings. In these two periods, human nature did not change, nor did the definitions of corrupt actions proscribed by the law and the administrators' code of conduct. But radical transformations in the political economy impinged on individuals, via their work units, and affected the prevalence and mode of corruption.

The classical socialist period, characterized by a low level of production, a high concentration of power at the top, and a weak criminal justice system, clearly had a lower incidence of corruption than was the case under reform socialism. In the latter period, there was higher production, a better standard of living, greater local authority, and a better established criminal justice system. This finding challenges the notion that attributes corruption to lack of resources, a high concentration of power, and the absence of an institutionalized criminal justice system, or at least requires serious qualification. Perhaps there is no objective standard of adequate resources. Perhaps it is not the scarcity but the perceived scarcity of supplies that motivates corruption. Perhaps it is not just the concentration of power at the top that leads to corruption, but rather the overlapping of power at any level. Perhaps it does not require a strong criminal justice system to stop crime, but rather an effective system of social control inherent within the work organizations to do so. An analysis of the Chinese situation between 1949 and 1989 seems to suggest that at the very least these modifications and specifications are necessary.

John Hagan has argued in his power-control theory that white collar crime is rooted in hierarchical class relations where perpetrators impose their power illicitly on others.[1] In the absence of private ownership, social differentiation in China, however, is based not on class as we understand it in the West, but on criteria stemming from power and privileges endowed by the state, which in turn are translated into a differential ranking system where influence is associated with office. Furthermore, as I tried to show, officials' propensity to abuse this power is contingent upon the ideological and structural patterns not just within the organization but beyond it.

The ideology of a society can both insulate or encourage corruption. For example, the egalitarian and idealistic orientations of socialism in its pure form tempered the drive for material gains and deterred corruption. But, at the same time, the competitive spirit and desire to conform and to produce benefits for the "collective" prompted individuals to resort to devious means to achieve collective and legitimate goals such as production targets. The situation is not unlike the Mertonian explanation of deviance[2]—that is, individuals and groups who want to achieve socially accepted goals but who cannot attain them through the legitimate channels turn to devious or illegitimate ones. These tensions in Chinese society are further enhanced by elements in the traditional culture that emphasized altruism and benevolence, on one hand, and reciprocity, particularistic ties, and face, on the other. The former were consistent with socialist ideals, but the latter condemned by the party.

Similarly, organizational structures can both encourage and deter corruption at the same time. Corruption is a violation of trust by those to whom responsibilities and power have been delegated. Every organization gives its administrators some freedom in the exercise of their responsibilities, but in so doing it also offers them opportunities to abuse these powers.[3] When the upper echelons put pressure on the lower levels to meet organizational goals, but do not provide adequate means to achieve these targets legitimately, they inadvertently encourage the use of devious means. In China, watchdog government agencies are supposed to anticipate and counter these tendencies. But because the government promotes organizational solidarity to boost morale and output, the virtue of loyalty often becomes the vice whereby internal and external investigations are thwarted or sabotaged. Attempts at uncovering abuses by monitoring agencies are further hampered because they typically have less power and fewer resources than the units they are investigating. These inherent organizational contradictions plagued Chinese bureaucracies even when they ostensibly exerted rigid controls.

Corruption is a symptom of ineffective integration or social control. For this reason, Travis Hirschi, and to some extent Hagan, argues that effective social control rests on the actors' commitment to the system, which in turn is affected by their closeness with the family, the assumption being that family and societal values overlap.[4] Complexities multiply, however, when family or particularistic values clash with political ideas. As I indicated in Chapter 5, despite official efforts to undermine, or more aptly, redirect loyalties from family to the state, the tension between the two spheres was never really resolved. Traditional values conflict with the communist ones, and loyalty to the family sometimes undermine commitment to the collective.

Incentives and opportunities for corruption are present even in a putatively monolithic and tightly controlled society like China. The prevalence of corruption, however, rests on the balance between the forces that encourage and discourage corruption within an organization, a balance that fluctuates with government policies at any particular time. The specific congeries of these forces within and outside the work organizations provide different moral restraints and incentives as well as opportunities and constraints which contributed to changes in corruption in the two periods.

Under classical socialism, the civil culture with its emphasis on altruism and probity, surrounded and reinforced the administrative subcultures, which in turn highlighted honesty, discipline, and self-denial. Despite the pressure to fulfill organizational targets—which could sometimes lead to breaking the rules,—the state employees' strong commitment to and trust in the socialist ideology were effective deterrents against more serious forms of corruption. In the sixties, however, the commitment was eroded by the uncertainties and excesses of the political campaigns. In the eighties, the government's endorsement of the contradictory values of socialism and capitalism created more confusion and dilemmas among administrators. According to the new materialistic ideology, administrators were expected to be altruistic and self-sacrificing, while their work units were to be operated on the profit principle. They were required to live frugally while society valued money, material acquisitions, and success. These disjunctions undermined the officials' commitment to socialism. They became self-interested and, in their confusion and disillusionment, sought refuge in the familiar traditional particularistic values and in the pursuit of financial security and personal comfort which seemed to promote corruption.

At the same time, the infrastructures both inside and outside the work organization offered administrators greater opportunities for corruption than during the classical socialist period. In a capitalist society, the striving for individual material gain is regulated by rules of acceptable behavior that are deeply ingrained in the culture and more or less implemented with structural safeguards. But in China the old rules of behavior became irrelevant, and new formal and informal norms of acceptable behaviors were not clearly defined. In this moral and normative vacuum, the means chosen were often the practical and not those formerly considered permissible or acceptable. As a result, corruption, which had been under control in the fifties, became a serious social problem in the eighties. Money assumed greater importance in these illicit exchanges, and the monetary values involved multiplied exponentially from a few yuan in the fifties to tens of thousands in the eighties. While many of the means administrators used to bilk the government and their clients remained largely the same throughout these forty years, the former became more varied and innovative as they learned to exploit the weaknesses in the socialist system and the loopholes in the capitalist one.

The close link between the political economy and corruption should not be surprising. Corruption is, after all, primarily a crime against property, and the economic structure within which goods are produced and distributed necessarily has a bearing on the opportunities for corruption and the means for carrying it out. The economy determines the value assigned to different goods, their availability, and their accessibility to different social groups. However, these patterns, especially in a socialist society, are not based on the invisible hand of the market operating according to the law of supply and demand. Even the market in capitalist countries is regulated to some extent by the government. In socialist countries, political leaders plan and organize the economy, delegate power and assign privileges to the different levels in government. The resulting socioeconomic organization affects the fabric of corruption—the power and resources accessible to dishonest administrators, the means used, and the nature of their corrupt practices.

The preference for material goods over cash, the proclivity for wasting public resources on the job rather than stealing them, the practice of hoarding and bartering materials, the submission of false reports, the speculation in state commodities, and, more recently, the speculation in stocks can all be traced to the way the economy is organized. Furthermore, any social exchange, whether corrupt or not, is an enactment of the relative power among the actors. Thus, in China during the eighties the distribution of power within organizations affected the prerogatives, authority, and actions of administrators. Some kinds of corruption, like bribery or extortion, were clear exercises of power over the victims; others, like bartering among organizations, reflected a more equitable but nevertheless asymmetrical relationship between organizations controlling different resources; and others, like false reporting, exposed the vulnerability of certain administrators vis-à-vis their superiors. But in every case, dishonest administrators made use of the power accompanying their positions within their organizations, as defined by the political economy of the larger society.

The political economic ethos find expression in the economic units. At the level of individual organizations and work units, the values and beliefs of leaders and followers come to the fore. For example: Are their subordinates viewed as wards to be protected or exploited? Does the interest of their unit take precedence over others? Are their superiors authorities to be obeyed and humored with false reports, or to be ignored and fooled by fraud and tax evasions? These political economic ethos also regulate the administrators' relationship with outside units, determining whether they should serve, cooperate with, or exploit them.

In short, these social and organizational conditions (1) provide the motivation or moral restraints on the basis of which officials can decide whether to indulge in corrupt behavior or not, and (2) structure the opportunities or hurdles accordingly. The balance between these different considerations shapes individual decisions with regard to the exercise of power, and in turn, the incidence and pattern of corruption in an organization at a particular time. That the incidence, forms, and patterns of corruption are deeply nested in the social organization of the work units and of the larger society helps to explain the changing forms of corruption in China, and the specific means employed.

Searching for Honest Governance

Is corruption inevitable in the transition to market socialism, a fact of economic and political life that will ultimately disappear or abate? Those who suggest that it will disappear when central planning gives way to a market economy are too optimistic. The prevalence of corruption in many developing nations of Africa, Asia, and South America fully integrated into the free market economy proves otherwise. The recent trend of developing corruption in China suggests that it may only gain momentum if left unchecked.

Various solutions have been proposed, for example, diluting the power of state officials, decentralizing economic decision making, or democratic reforms. But these seem impractical, at least in the short run. This is not to argue against popular participation; but the lesson from Russia is worth noting. Hasty political reforms can bring disastrous consequences. It is difficult to make cross national comparisons on crime and especially corruption, yet one gets the impression that the problem is more severe in Russia than China which may have been the result of the uncertainty, the power vacuum, and the breakdown of social control generated by Gorbachev's liberalization policies.

If I am even partially correct in assuming that the growth of corruption is an upshot of the new political economic infrastructures which affect the way state officials exercise their power, then a comprehensive solution is required. Development is a complex process that brings unintended consequences—the proliferation of corruption in China is one example. But the problem of corruption is necessarily subordinate to the larger developmental goals of raising national production, improving the population's standard of living, and ensuring political stability. The existing policies seem to be producing overall satisfactory results, and are unlikely to change. Solutions to corruption have to start from this premise.

The solution to corruption requires a practical remedy at all levels in which existing and potential contradictions with regard to means and ends within and between sectors are identified and resolved. Priorities have to be established and choices have to be made. If honest government is the goal, then this strategy calls for revising the official culture by substituting practical goals, reasonable expectations, and guidelines of behavior for state employees for the current idealistic and unrealistic political rhetoric. Measures have to be taken to reduce or eliminate the profitability of corruption, such as, the elimination of the dual pricing system. The government has to be continuously vigilant because economic policies will change and new opportunities for corruption will arise. To deter the gray corruption characteristic of socialist systems, administrators should be provided with adequate resources and supportive infrastructures to fulfill organizational objectives. Only a bureaucracy with a coherent organizational culture and effective resources to fulfill its mandate can inspire its members to follow organizational rules in the exercise of their authorities and prerogatives to attain meaningful and attainable goals.

If corruption is generated by social arrangements, then to control it relies much less on current punitive measures than on positive incentives. The more effective rule in the past has rested on a well-integrated social system under a putatively honest leadership in the absence of an established criminal justice system. Draconian measures from a Western style criminal justice system might not resolve the problem. Harsh punishments do not necessarily deter criminals.[5] Severe sentences meted out during the anti-corruption campaigns have not produced any long term controlling effect.[6]

Effective law enforcement agencies do not need to use their punitive powers; their presence deters would-be perpetrators. But these monitoring agencies need to be staffed not just by a disciplined corp loyal to the political leaders, but by trained professionals dedicated to honest governance. They have to function free from political intervention and vested with adequate resources and power to oversee the operation of the work units at all levels.

Chinese citizens look to their leaders for guidance; honesty and dedication especially of the top leaders during the classical socialist period have trickled down to inspire those below to do likewise. Curbing corruption therefore calls for exemplary behavior from the leaders at every level. A truly compelling approach to the ideal honest governance would encourage and reward exemplars of upright officials and work units, and punish officials —even at the highest levels—and their family members who have engaged in corruption. Enforcing laws universally would convince the population of its sanctity and is more effective than any propaganda or legal education campaign. It will probably be only then that the public and the growing number of private administrators will follow organizational rules and laws, and refrain from employing public or private property for personal gain. Or to use the jargon once favored by the Chinese Communist government, only then will state cadres integrate the theory with the practice of honest governance.

Notes

1. John Hagan, *Structural Criminology* (New Brunswick: Rutgers University Press, 1989).

2. Susan Shirk, *Competititve Comrades: Career Incentives and Student Strategies* (Berkeley: University of California Press, 1982); Robert King Merton, *Social Theory and Social Structure* (Glencoe, Ill: Free Press, 1957).

3. Susan P. Shapiro, "Collaring the crime, not the criminal: reconsidering the concept of white collar crime," *American Sociological Review* 55 (June 1990): 346–365.

4. Travis Hirschi, *Causes of Delinquency* (Berkeley: University of California Press, 1969); Hagan, op. cit.

5. S.S. Brier and S.E. Fienberg, "Recent Econometric Modelling of Crime and Punishment: Support for the Deterrence Hypothesis?" *Evaluation Review* 4 (1980), pp. 147–191; Jack Gibbs, *Crime, Punishment and Deterrence* (New York: Elsevier, 1975).

6. Information gathered from interviews in summer 1995.

Glossary

baohu san	保护伞
benwei zhuyi	本位主义
bu zheng zhi feng	不正之风
chiku	吃苦
da chi da he	大吃大喝
daoqie	盗窃
Deng Xiaoping	邓小平
difang zhuyi	地方主义
dian ba	电霸
duli wangguo	独立王国
fubai	腐败

fuhua	腐化
fu-mu guan	父母官
ganbu	干部
Gansu	甘肃
gongsi fa	公司法
guan dao	官倒
guanliao zhuyi	官僚主义
guan guan xiang hu	官官相护
guanxi hu	关系户
guan zi liang ge kou	官字两个口
Guomindang	国民党
haochu	好处
Heilongjiang	黑龙江
jia gong ji si	假公济私
junzi	君子

lao yundong yuan	老运动员
lingdao ganbu	领导干部
Liu Shaoqi	刘少奇
Mao Zedong	毛泽东
meiyou renqing wei	没有人情味
mu	亩
nuoyong	挪用
pian qu	骗取
qiangduo	抢夺
qiangjie	抢劫
qiang suo	抢索
qintun	侵吞
Qing	清
shantou zhuyi	山头主义
shang xing xia xiao	上行下效

shenghuo	生活
shou huilu	受贿赂
Sichuan	四川
suo hui	索贿
tanwu	贪污
tao qu	套取
Tian'anmen	天安门
touji daoba	投机倒把
xian	县
xiang	乡
xin fang	信访
xingzheng fa	行政法
xingzheng ganbu	行政干部
yiban ganbu	一般干部
yi quan mou si	以权谋私

yiwofeng	一窝蜂
yiyuanhua lingdao	一元化领导
zhapian	诈骗
zousi	走私
zu	组

Selected Bibliography

General Works on Corruption

Bayley, David. "The Effect of Corruption in Developing Nations." *Western Political Quarterly* 19, no. 4 (December 1966): 719–32.

Becker, Gary S., and George J. Stigler. "Law Enforcement, Malfeasance, and Compensation of Enforcers." *Journal of Legal Studies* 3, no. 1 (January 1974): 1–17.

Belshaw, Cyril S. *Traditional Exchange and Modern Markets*. Englewood Cliffs, N.J.: Prentice Hall, 1965.

Biderman, A.D., and J.P. Lynch. *Understanding Crime Incidence Statistics: Why the UCR Diverges from the NCS*. New York: Springer-Verlag, 1991.

Braithwaite, John. "Transnational Corporations and Corruption: Towards Some International Solutions." *International Journal of the Sociology of Law* 7, no. 2 (May 1979): 125–42.

Brier, S.S., and S.E. Fienberg, "Recent Econometric Modelling of Crime and Punishment: Support for the Deterrence Hypothesis?" *Evaluation Review* 4, no. 1 (February 1980): 147–91.

Cheal, David. *The Gift Economy*. London: Routledge, 1988.

Clarke, Michael. *Business Crime: Its Nature and Control*. New York: St. Martin's Press, 1990.

———. *Corruption: Cases, Consequences and Control*. New York: St. Martin's Press, 1983.

Djilas, Milovan. *The New Class: An Analysis of the Communist System*. New York: Praeger, 1957.

Gardiner, John. *The Politics of Corruption*. Beverly Hills: Russell Sage, 1970.

Galasi, Peter, and Gabor Kertesi. "Rat Race and Equilibria in Markets with Side Payments Under Socialism." *Acta Oeconomica* 41, nos. 3/4 (1989): 267–92.

———. "The Spread of Bribery in a Centrally Planned Economy." *Acta Oeconomica* 38, nos. 3/4 (1987): 371–89.

Gibbs, Jack. *Crime, Punishment and Deterrence*. New York: Elsevier, 1975.

Giddens, Anthony. *The Constitution of Society: Outline of the Theory of Structuration*. Berkeley: University of California Press, 1984.

Green, Gary. *Occupational Crime*. Chicago: Nelson Hall, 1990.

Grossman, Gregory. "The Second Economy in the USSR." *Problems of Communism* 26, no. 5 (September-October 1977): 25–40.

Hagan, John. *Structural Criminology.* New Brunswick, N.J.: Rutgers University Press, 1989.

Handelman, Stephen. *Comrade Criminal.* New Haven: Yale University Press, 1995.

Heidenheimer, Arnold J. *Political Corruption: Readings in Comparative Analysis.* New Brunswick, N.J.: Transaction Books, 1978.

Heidenheimer, Arnold J., Michael Johnston, and Victor T. Levine. *Political Corruption: A Handbook.* New Brunswick, N.J.: Transaction Books, 1990.

Heiland, Hans-gunther, Louis I. Shelley, and Hisao Katoh, eds. *Crime and Control in Comparative Perspectives.* New York: Walter de Gruyter, 1992.

Herbert, E. Alexander, et al. *The Politics and Economics of Organized Crime.* Lexington, Mass.: Lexington Press, 1985.

Herbert, David L., and Howard Tritt. *Corporation of Corruption.* Springfield, Ill.: Thomas, 1984.

Hirschi, Travis. *Causes of Delinquency.* Berkeley: University of California Press, 1969.

Humphrey, Caroline, and Stephen Hugh-Jones. *Barter, Exchange and Value: An Anthropological Approach.* Cambridge: Cambridge University Press, 1992.

Jogannathan, N. Vijjay. *Informal Markets in Developing Countries.* New York: Oxford University Press, 1987.

Johnston, Michael, "The Political Consequences of Corruption," *Comparative Politics* 18, no. 4 (July 1986): 459–77.

Klitgaard, Robert E. *Corruption in Developing Countries.* Berkeley: University of California Press, 1988.

Kornai, Janos. *The Socialist System: The Political Economy of Communism.* Princeton: Princeton University Press, 1992.

Krueger, Anne O. "The Political Economy of the Rent-Seeking Society." *American Economic Review* 64 (June 1974): 291–303.

Leff, Nathaniel H. "Economic Development Through Bureaucratic Corruption." *American Behavioral Scientist* 8, no. 3 (November 1964): 8–14.

Los, Maria. "Crime and Economy in the Communist Countries." In *White Collar and Economic Crime: Multidisciplinary and Cross-National Perspective,* ed. Peter Wickman and Timothy Dailey, pp. 121–38. Lexington, Mass.: Lexington Books, 1982.

———. "Dynamic Relationships of the First and Second Economies in Old and New Marxist States." In *The Second Economy in Marxist State,* ed. Maria Los, pp. 193–231. New York: St. Martin's Press, 1990.

MacKenzie, Doris Layton, Phyllis T. Baunach, and Roy R. Roberg. *Measuring Crime Large Scale, Long Range Efforts.* Albany: State University of New York Press, 1990.

Mauss, Marcel. *The Gift: The Form and Reason for Exchange in Archaic Societies.* Translated by W.D. Halls. New York: W.W. Norton, 1950.

Merton, Robert King. *Social Theory and Social Structure.* Glencoe, Ill.: Free Press, 1957.

Nye, J.S. "Corruption and Political Development: A Cost-Benefit Analysis." *American Political Science Review* 61, no. 2 (June 1967): 417–27.

O'Brien, Robert. *Crime and Victimization Data.* Beverly Hills: Sage, 1985.

Poveda, Tony G. *Rethinking White Collar Crime.* Westport, Conn.: Praeger, 1994.

Quinney, R. *Class, State and Crime.* New York: MacKay, 1977.

Reynolds, Morgan. *Crime By Choice: An Economic Analysis.* Dallas: Fisher Institute, 1985.

Roener, Michael, and Christine Jones. *Markets in Developing Countries: Parallel, Fragmented and Black.* Lanham, Md.: ICS Press, 1991.

Rose-Ackerman, Susan. *Corruption: A Study in Political Economy.* New York: Academic Press, 1978.

Saney, Parvitz. *Crime and Culture in America.* New York: Greenwood, 1986.

Schwartz, Charles A. "Corruption and Poltical Development in the USSR." *Comparative Politics* 11, no. 4 (July 1979): 425–43.

Scott, James C., *Comparative Political Corruption.* Englewood Cliffs, N.J.: Prentice Hall, 1972.

Schmidt, Steffen W., Laura Guasti, Carl Lande, and James C. Scott. *Friends, Followers and Factions: A Reader in Political Clientelism.* Berkeley: University of California Press, 1977.

Shapiro, Susan P. "Collaring the Crime, Not the Criminal: Reconsidering the Concept of White Collar Crime." *American Sociological Review* 55 (June 1990): 346–65.

Shelley, Louise I. *Crime and Modernization: The Impact of Industrialization and Urbanization on Crime.* Cardondale, Ill.: South Illinois University Press, 1981.

Sutherland, E.H. *White Collar Crime.* New York: Holt Rinehart, 1961.

Theobald, Robin. *Corruption, Development and Underdevelopment.* Durham, N.C.: Duke University Press, 1990.

Tilman, Robert O. "Emergence of Black-Market Bureaucracy, Administration and Corruption in the New States." *Public Administration Review* 28, no. 5 (September/October 1968): 437–44.

Wickman, Peter, and Timothy Dailey. *White Collar and Economic Crime.* Lexington, Mass.: Lexington Books, 1982.

Wraith, Ronald, and Edgar Simpkins. *Corruption in Developing Countries.* New York: Norton, 1963.

General Works on China

Barnett, A. Doak. *China on the Eve of Communist Takeover.* New York: Frederick A. Praeger, 1963.

———. *Chinese Communist Politics in Action.* Seattle: University of Washington Press, 1969.

———. *Communist China: The Early Years, 1949–55.* New York: Frederick A. Praeger, 1964.

Bianco, Lucien. *Origins of the Chinese Revolution, 1915–1949.* Stanford: Stanford University Press, 1971.

Bian Yanjie. *Work and Inequality in Urban China.* Albany, N.Y.: State University of New York Press, 1994.

Brugger, Bill. *China: Liberation and Transformation, 1942–1962.* London: Croom Helm, 1981.

Bruun, Ole. *Business and Bureaucracy in a Chinese City: An Ethnography of Private Business Households in Contemporary China.* Berkeley: University of California, Institute of Asian Studies, 1993.

Burton, Charles. *Political and Social Change in China Since 1978.* Westport, Conn.: Greenwood Press, 1990.

Cell, Charles. *Revolution at Work: Mobilization Campaigns in China.* New York: Academic Press, 1977.

Chan, Anita, Richard Madsen, and Jonathan Unger. *Chen Village Under Mao and Deng.* Berkeley: University of California Press, 1992.

Chi, Hsi-sheng. *Politics of Disillusionment: The Chinese Communist Party Under Deng Xiaoping 1978–1989.* Armonk, N.Y.: M.E. Sharpe, 1991.

Chu, Godwin C., and Francis L.K. Hsu. *Moving A Mountain: Cultural Change in China.* Honolulu: University of Hawaii, East-West Center, 1979.

Eastman, Lloyd E. *Seeds of Destruction: Nationalist China in War and Revolution, 1937–1949.* Stanford: Stanford University Press, 1984.

Eckstein, Alexander. *China's Economic Development.* Ann Arbor: University of Michigan Press, 1985.

Ethridge, James M. *China's Unfinished Revolution: Problems and Prospects Since Mao.* San Francisco: China Books and Periodicals, 1990.

Friedman, Edward, Paul G. Pickowicz, and Mark Selden, Kay Ann Johnson. *Chinese Village, Socialist State.* New Haven: Yale University Press, 1991.

Goodman, David, and Gerald Segal. *China at Forty: Mid-Life Crisis?* Oxford: Clarendon, 1989.

Han, Suyin. *Eldest Son: Zhou Enlai and the Making of Modern China.* New York: Hull and Wang, 1994.

Harrison, James Pinckney. *The Long March to Power: A History of the Chinese Communist Party, 1921–1972.* New York: Praeger, 1972.

Howe, Christopher. *China's Economy: A Basic Guide.* London: Paul Elek, 1978.

Huang, Shu-min. *The Spiral Road: Changes in a Chinese Village Through the Eyes of a Communist Party Leader.* Boulder: Westview Press, 1989.

Hwang Kwang-kuo. "Face and Favor: The Chinese Power Game." *American Journal of Sociology* 92, no. 4 (January 1987): 944–74.

Lardy, Nicholas. *Economic Growth and Distribution in China.* Cambridge: Cambridge University Press, 1978.

Lee, Keun. *Chinese Firms and the State in Transition: Property Rights and Agency Problems in the Reform Era.* Armonk, N.Y.: M.E. Sharpe, 1991.

Lee, Peter N.S. *Industrial Management and Economic Reform in China, 1949–1984.* Oxford: Oxford University Press, 1987.

Leng, Shao-chuan, ed. *Changes in China: Party, State, and Society.* Lanham, Md.: University Press of America, 1989.

Lewis, John Wilson. *Leadership in Communist China.* Ithaca: Cornell University Press, 1963.

Li Zhisui. *The Private Life of Chairman Mao*. New York: Random House, 1994.

Lin Wei and Arnold Chao. *China's Economic Reforms*. Philadelphia: University of Pennsylvania Press, 1982.

MacFarquhar, Roderick. *The Hundred Flowers Campaign and the Chinese Intellectuals*. New York: Octagon Books, 1974.

Madsen, Richard. *Morality and Power in a Chinese Village*. Berkeley: University of California Press, 1984.

Marx, Karl. *The Communist Manifesto*. London: Penguin, 1985.

———. *Essential Writings of Karl Marx*. New York: Macmillan, 1987.

———. *Karl Marx: Economy, Class and Social Revolution*. New York: Scribner, 1975.

———. *Karl Marx: On Society and Social Change*. Chicago: University of Chicago Press, 1973.

Maxwell, Neville, and Bruce McFarlane. *China's Changed Road to Development*. Oxford: Pergamon Press, 1984.

McCormick, Barrett C. *Political Reform in Post-Mao China: Democracy and Bureaucracy in a Leninist State*. Berkeley: University of California Press, 1990.

Mercer, Thomas A. *The Internal Organization of Ch'ing Bureaucracy*. Cambridge, Mass.: Harvard University Press, 1973.

Miyashita, Tadao. *The Currency and Financial System of Mainland China*. Washington: University of Washington Press, 1966.

Odgaard, Ole. *Private Enterprises in Rural China: Impact on Agriculture and Social Stratification*. Hong Kong: Avebury, 1992.

Ogden, Suzanne. *China's Unresolved Issues: Politics, Development, and Culture*. Englewood Cliffs, N.J.: Prentice Hall, 1989

Oi, Jean C. *State and Peasant in Contemporary China: The Political Economy of Village Government*. Berkeley: University of California Press, 1989.

Pepper, Suzanne. *Civil War in China: The Political Struggle, 1945–1949*. Berkeley: University of California Press, 1978.

Reynolds, Bruce L., ed. *Chinese Economic Reform: How Far, How Fast?* New York: Academic Press, 1988.

Reynolds, Bruce L., and Ilpyong J. Kim, *China's Economic Policy: Economic Reform at Midstream*. New York: Paragon House, 1988.

Riskin, Carl. *China's Political Economy*. Oxford: Oxford University Press, 1987.

Rodzinski, Witold. *The People's Republic of China: A Concise Political History*. New York: Free Press 1988.

Saich, Tony. *China: Politics and Government*. New York: St. Martin's Press, 1981.

Ruan Ming. *Deng Xiaoping: Chronicle of an Empire*. Boulder: Westview Press, 1994.

Schurmann, Franz. *Ideology and Organization in Communist China*. Berkeley: University of California Press, 1968.

Shirk, Susan L. *Competitive Comrades: Career Incentives and Student Strategies*. Berkeley: University of California Press, 1982.

Shue, Vivienne. *The Reach of the State.* Stanford: Stanford University Press, 1988.
Siu, Helen F. *Agents and Victims in South China: Accomplices in Rural Revolution.* New Haven: Yale University Press, 1989.
Solinger, Dorothy. *Chinese Business Under Socialism: The Politics of Domestic Commerce, 1949–1980.* Berkeley: University of California Press, 1984.
Tennien, Mark. *No Secret Is Safe: Behind the Bamboo Curtain.* New York: Farrar, Straus, and Young, 1952.
Thurston, Anne F. *A Chinese Odyssey: The Life and Times of a Chinese Dissident.* New York: Charles Scribner's Sons, 1991.
Tung, S.T. *Secret Diary from Red China.* Indianapolis, Ind.: Bobbs-Merrill, 1961.
Utley, Peter. *Last Chance in China.* New York: Bobbs-Merrill, 1947.
Uhalley, Stephen, Jr. *A History of the Chinese Communist Party.* Stanford: Stanford University, Hoover Institute, 1988.
Walder, Andrew G. *Communist Neo-Traditionalism: Work and Authority in Chinese Industry.* Berkeley: University of California Press, 1986.
———. "Career Mobility and the Communist Political Order." *American Sociological Review* 60 (June 1995): 309–28.
Waller, Derek J. *The Government and Politics of the People's Republic of China.* London: Hutchinson, 1981.
Wei Lin, and Arnold Chao, ed. *China's Economic Reforms.* Philadelphia: University of Pennsylvania Press, 1982.
Wilson, Richard, and Amy Wilson, eds. *Organizational Behavior in Chinese Society.* New York: Praeger, 1981.
Wu Han. *Lishi De Jinzi. The Mirror of History.* Chongqing: Shen Shen Chubanshe, 1945.
Wu Jinglian, and Zhao Renwei. "The Dual Pricing System in China's Industry." In *Chinese Economic Reform: How Far, How Fast,* ed., Bruce L. Reynolds, pp. 19–28. Boston: Academic Press, 1988.
Xue Muqiao. *China Between Plan and Market.* Washington. D.C.: World Bank, 1990.
———. *China's Socialist Economy.* Beijing: Foreign Languages Press, 1981.
———. *Ten Great Years.* Beijing: Foreign Languages Press, 1960.

Works on Law and Crime in China

Bi Xiaonan. *Lun Fanzui Wenti De Shehui Xing* (Discussion on the social root of crime) *Shenhui* 4 (1983): 4–7.
Blaustein, Albert P. *Fundamental Legal Documents of Communist China.* South Hackensack, N.J.: Rothman, 1962.
Bodde, Derk, and Clarence Morris. *Law in Imperial China: Exemplified by 190 Ch'ing Dynasty Cases.* Philadelphia: University of Pennsylvania Press, 1967.
Chan, Anita, and Jonathan Unger. "Gray and Black: The Hidden Economy in Rural China." *Pacific Affairs* 55 (Fall 1982): 452–71.
Chen Nai-Chao. *Zhonggong Tanwu Jiantao.* (An examination of corruption in Communist China.) Hong Kong: Xin Shiji Chubanshe, 1953.

Chen, Phillip M. *Law and Justice: The Legal System in China, 2400* B.C. to A.D. 1960. New York: Dunnellen Publishing, 1973
Cohen, Jerome A. "Chinese Mediation on the Eve of Modernization." *California Law Review* 54, no. 3 (August 1966): 1201–1226.
———. *Contemporary Chinese Law: Research Problems and Perspectives.* Cambridge, Mass.: Harvard University Press, 1970.
———. "The Criminal Process in the People's Republic of China." *Harvard Law Review* 79, no. 3 (January 1966): 469–533.
———. *The Criminal Process in the People's Republic of China, 1949–1963: An Introduction.* Cambridge, Mass.: Harvard University Press, 1968.
do Rosario, Louise, "Big Four, Less One." *Far Eastern Economic Review* (November 17, 1988): 91–92
Gao Gang. *Fandui Tanwu Tuihua, Fandui Guanliao Zhuyi* (Oppose the acceleration of corruption, oppose bureaucratism). Guangzhou: Huanan Renmin Chubanshe, 1952.
Gates, Hill. "Eating for Revenge: Consumption and Corruption Under Economic De-Reform." *Dialectical Anthropology* 16 (1991): 233–49.
Gong Ting. *The Politics of Corruption in Contemporary China.* Westport, Conn.: Praeger, 1994.
Harris, Peter. "Socialist Graft: The Soviet Union and the People's Republic of China—A Preliminary Survey." *Corruption and Reform* 1 (1986): 13–32.
He Bingsong. "Crime and Control in China." In *Crime and Control in Comparative Perspective,* ed. Hans-Gunther Heiland, Louis I. Shelley, and Hisa Katoh, pp. 241–57. New York: Walter de Gruyter, 1992.
Huang Weiding. *Zhongguo de Yinxing Jingji* (The hidden economy of China). Beijing: Zhongguo Shangye Chubanshe, 1992.
Kolenda, Helena. "One Party, Two Systems: Corruption in the People's Republic of China and Attempts to Control it." *Journal of Chinese Law* 4, no. 2 (Fall 1990): 189–232.
Lee, Peter Nan-shong. "Bureaucratic Corruption During the Deng Xiaoping Era." *Corruption and Reform* 5 (1990): 29–47.
Leng, Shao-chuan. *Justice in Communist China: A Survey of the Judicial System of the People's Republic of China.* Dobbs Ferry, N.Y.: Oceana Publications, 1967.
Lin, Robert H. "Criminal Law and Corruption in China." *New York Law School Journal of International and Comparative Law* 10, no. 1 (1989): 1–11.
Liu, Alan P.L. "The Politics of Corruption in the People's Republic of China." *American Political Science Review* 77, no. 3 (September 1983): 602–23.
Lubman, Stanley. "Mao and Mediation." *California Law Review* 55, no. 5 (November 1967): 1284–1359.
Meaney, Connie Squires. "Market Reform and Disintegrative Corruption in Urban China." In *Reform and Reaction in Post-Mao China: The Road to Tiananmen,* ed. Richard Baum, pp. 124–42. New York: Routledge 1991.
Meng Qinghua, and Zhao Yuanlong. *Dao Ye Bai Tai* (The speculators). Haerbin: Beifang Wenyi Chubanshe, 1991.
Oi, Jean C. "Market Reforms and Corruption in Rural China." In *Reform and*

Reaction in Post-Mao China: The Road to Tian'anmen, ed. Richard Baum, pp. 143–61. New York: Routledge, 1991.

Ostergaard, Clemens Stubbe. "Explaining China's Recent Political Corruption: Patterns, Remedies and Counter Strategies at the Local Level." *Corruption and Reform* 1 (1986): 209–33.

Ostergaard, Clemens Stubbe, and Christina Petersen. "Official Profiteering and the Tiananmen Square Demonstrations in China." *Corruption and Reform* 6 (1991): 87–107.

Ouyang Tao, Cui Qingsen, and Lei Yang. *Jingji Lingyu Yanzhong Fanzui Wenti Tanjiu* (An exploration into serious economic crimes). Beijing: Falü Chubanse, 1984.

Rocca, Jean Louis. "Corruption and Its Shadow: An Anthropological View of Corruption in China." *China Quarterly,* no. 130 (June 1992): 402–16.

Sun Lijin, and Liu Renhua. "Fanzui de kexue jishi" (Foundation stone of the science of criminology). *Shehiu Kexue,* no. 4 (1983): 84–106.

Rojek, Dean G. "Changing Directions of Chinese Social Control." In *Comparative Criminal Justice: Traditional and Non-traditional Systems of Law and Control,* ed. Charles B. Fields, and Richter H. Moore Jr., pp. 234–49. Prospect Heights, Ill.: Waveland Press, 1956.

Wang, Zuofu. *Zhongguo Falü Yanjiu* (Chinese law research). Beijing: Zhongguo Renmin Daxue Chubanshe, 1988.

Wang Zhimin, and Huang Jingping. *Jingji Fazhan yu Fanzui Bianhua* (Changes in the economy and crime). Beijing: Zhongguo Renmin Daxue Chubanshe, 1991.

Weng, Byron, S.J., and Hsin Chang. *Introduction to Chinese Law.* Hong Kong: Ming Pao Publishing, 1989.

White, Gordon. "Corruption and the Transition from Socialism in China" *Journal of Law and Society* 23, no. 1 (March 1996): 149–69.

White, Lynn T. "Changing Concepts of Corruption in Communist China: Early 1950s Versus Early 1980s." In *Changes and Continuities in Chinese Communism,* vol. 2, ed. Shaw Yu-ming, pp. 316–53. Boulder: Westview Press, 1988.

World Bank. *China Between Plan and Market.* Washington, D.C.: World Bank, 1990.

Yang, Mayfair Mei-hui. "The Gift Economy and State Power in China." *Comparative Studies in Society and History* 31, no. 1 (January 1989): 25–54.

———. *Gifts, Favors, and Banquets: The Art of Social Relationships in China.* Ithaca: Cornell University Press, 1994.

Jiaji Shehui Tizhi Bijiao Bianji Bu. *Fubai: Huobi yu Zhuanli de Jiaowen* (Corruption: The exchange of money and power). Beijing: Zhongguo Jiangwen Chubanshe, 1989.

Zhang Huangguang. *Zhonghua Renmin Gongheguo Xin Zheng Fa Gi Liao Xuanbian* (Selections of administrative laws in the People's Republic of China). Beijing: Qunzhong Chubanshe, 1984.

Zhonggong Zhongyang Jilu Jiancha Weiyuan hui Yanjiushi. *Shenru Chijiu Fan Fubai* (Fight hard and persistently against corruption). Beijing: Zhongguo Zhengfang Chubanshe, 1989.

Zuiggao Renmin Jianchayuan Bianjizu. *Zhongda Tanwu Shouhui Duzhi Zuian Anli Xuanbian* (Selection of important cases of corruption and dereliction of duties). Beijing: Zhongguo Zhengfa Daxue Chubanshe, 1989.

Chiao Chu Guandao Anjian Shi Yung Fa Lü Shouce (A practical handbook in investigating cases of speculation). Beijing: Falü Chubanshe, 1989.

Jingji Shenpan Shouce (Handbook on the evaluation of the Economy). Beijing: Renmin Fayuan Chubanshe, 1987.

Lianzheng Jianshe Shouce (Handbook to build an honest government). Chengdu: Sichuan Renmin Chubanshe, 1989.

Renmin Fayuan Anlixuan (Selection of cases from the People's court), vol. 1–9. Beijing: Renmin Fayuan Chubanshe, 1994.

Xing Shi Fanzui Anli Congshu (Selections of criminal cases). Beijing: Zhongguo Jiancha Chubanshe, 1991.

Reference Works

Black, Henry Cambell. *Black's Law Dictionary*. St. Paul, Minn.: West Publishing, 1979.

China's Statistical Abstract, 1989.. New York: Praeger, 1989.

The Criminal Law and the Criminal Procedure Law of the People's Republic of China. Beijing: Foreign Languages Press, 1984.

International Monetary Fund. *International Financial Statistics*. Washington, D.C.: International Monetary Fund, Annual.

People's Supreme Court Annual Report.

Zhonghua Renmin Gongheguo Xing Zheng Ziliao Xuanbian (Selections of administrative law in the People's Republic of China). Beijing: Qunzhong Chubanshe, 1984.

Zhonghua Renmin Gongheguo Xing Zheng Su Song Fa (Administrative procedural law of the People's Republic of China). Beijing: Zhongguo Min Zhu Fazhi Chubanshe, 1989.

Zhongguo Tongji Nianjian (Statistical yearbook of China). Beijing: People's Republic of China Statistical Bureau, Annual.

Anhui Ribao

Dongxi

Far Eastern Economic Review

Guangming Ribao

Nineties

Renmin Ribao

Shaanxi Ribao

Sichuan Daily

Statistical Abstract of the United States. Washington, D.C.: U.S. Department of Commerce.

Tsangming

Zhongguo Falu Yanjui

Zhongguo Nianbao

Index

Xinfang (anonymous reporting of irregularities), 102
Xingzheng fa (administrative laws/codes), 7
Xingzheng ganbu (administrative cadres), 11
Xingzheng renyuan (administrative personnel), 11

Yang, Mayfair M., 52, 108
Ye Jianying, 35
Yi wo feng (moving in the same direction), 119
Yiban ganbu (ordinary cadres), 11

Yiyuanhua lingdao (chain of command), 36, 52
Young Communist League, 130
Young Pioneers, 130
Yuchuan mou shi (corruption of power), 3

Zhang Shiyan, 93, 124
Zhao Ziyang, 40
Zhapian (fraud), 14–15
Zousi fan (smugglers), 16
Zousi (smuggling), 16
Zu (team unit), 41

Julia Kwong is professor of sociology at the University of Manitoba. She has authored a number of books and articles on contemporary China. Her book *Cultural Revolution in China's Schools* received the 1989 book of the year award from the American Educational Studies Association.